STORM

A Memoir

IAN HUGHES

Copyrights

Storm Child © Ian Hughes, 2025

All rights reserved. No part of this book may be reproduced, stored in a retrieval system, or transmitted in any.
form or by any means—electronic, mechanical, photocopying, recording, or otherwise—without the prior written permission of the author.

This book is a work of non-fiction. The events and experiences described are based on the author's memories
and accounts. Some names and identifying details have been changed to protect the privacy of individuals.

Published by Ian Hughes

ISBN: 9781068239007

Printed in the United Kingdom

British English edition

First Edition: 2025

Dedication

For those who weathered the storm—and those still learning how to dance in the rain.

Praise for Storm Child

"A gripping and lyrical journey through hardship and healing."

— E. Tate

"Raw, honest, unforgettable."

— S. Hughes

Preface

This book is not an easy one to read—and it was never an easy one to live.

But every page is stitched with truth.

Some memories are loud. Others whisper through the years. I wrote Storm Child not to tell a perfect story, but an honest one.

May it find the ones who need it.

Table of Contents

Copyrights 2
Dedication 3
Preface 4
Table of Contents 5
Acknowledgement 9

    Prologue 1

    Born in the Storm 2

    Early Wanderings 6

    School Daze 12

    If I can't have you, no one will. 15

    They Broke the Kids' Code 21

    A Night in the Park 24

    My Grand Fathers Garden 28

    Moving Back to My Hometown 33

    Another Day to my Ravine 39

    Fists Clenched at My Side 43

    The Bull in the Field 49

    Treasure Island and Kidnapped 54

Into Care	61
I Couldn't Even Take My Books	66
Distrust Misplaced	71
Gratitude and Reflection	73
Changes	75
Brief Paradise	79
The Broken Bank	83
Back to Nothing	87
The White Building	92
Rules Rules and More Rules	98
The Day Elvis Died	103
The Flight	110
Caught and Punished	117
The Christmas Miracle	120
Glencoe	124
The Weight of Shame	128
The Adult Amnesia	131
No Way Hosea	134
Freedom	138

The Coal Bing	140
Lady Hamilton's Estate	144
The Ruins of Chatelherault	147
Cadzow Castle	151
The Blue Waters	155
The Tunnel at the Nature Trail	159
The Loch Lomond Adventure	163
Scrumping	166
Learning the Hard Way	169
Young Love	172
The First Step	174
My Grand Mother	177
Broken Twice	181
Chapter 45	184
Detonators	187
Cheap Cider	191
Smoke and Swagger	195
Psychobilly	198
Snakeskin Boots	201

Chapter 51	204
The Journey In	207
The Morning After	211
A New Chapter	214
Full Circle	217
Missing Photographs	221
The First Real Photograph	224
Scars Into Stars	226
The Invisible Battle	229
Thanks, and Reflections	232
Hopes and Dreams	235
About the Author	245
Support and Resources	246
1. Trauma-Informed Lens: Core Principles	250
2. For Book Groups / Workshops	251
3. For Professionals (Social Work, Education, Mental Health)	253
4. Additional Resources	254
5. Contact & Permissions	255

Acknowledgement

To my siblings, whose strength and perseverance have always inspired me.

To my grandparents, especially my grandfathers, who taught me the value of patience, hard work, and love. To my foster parents, who gave me a glimpse of what safety and warmth could feel like.

To the gentleman with the greenhouse full of tomatoes, whose quiet sanctuary offered me solace in a turbulent world.

And to all the storm children out there this too will pass. You are stronger than you know. Thank you for allowing me to share my story with you.

Prologue

In the eye of a storm, there is a calm, a place where the world stands still. It was during Scotland's fiercest storm of the century that my life began, born into a world that seemed to test my resolve from the very start. This memoir is not just a story of survival but a testament to the strength of the human spirit. Through the storms of childhood, the gales of loss, and the tempests of healing, I found my way. This is my story a storm child's journey through the squalls of life and into the light.

Chapter 1

Born in the Storm

The glass panes rattled like tambourines in a fury, the storm howling with a force that seemed deliberate as though the world itself was holding its breath. On January 15, 1968, Scotland's fiercest storm of the century tore through the land, and my father was in the heart of it. The wind screamed at 140 mph, the earth groaning beneath it. Slate tiles tumbled from rooftops like deadly raindrops, while ancient trees, their roots groaning in protest, were torn from the ground. Natures wrath was unyielding, and somewhere within it, my father, as young and determined as the storm itself, fought forward, determined to reach my mother. He trudged through the wreckage, each step a struggle against the howling gusts that seemed to tear at him. His coat, pulled tight against the bitter wind, flapped like a flag in a battle. The streets were littered with debris fallen power lines, upturned cars, chunks of roof tiles scattered like broken memories. In the distance, the faint glow of emergency lights flickered, but they seemed as distant as stars, lost in the storm's fury.

The wind howled around him, relentless, as if the very elements conspired to turn him back. It was a battle he was determined to win, though the path ahead was unclear. Every gust of wind, each blast of icy rain felt like a punishment. But still, he pressed forward. His breath came out in heavy clouds, freezing instantly in the bitter night air. His sixteen-mile journey to the hospital was lit only by the flickering lights of distant candles and the dim shadows of the wreckage around him. Each step forward felt like a small victory against the storm, against the world, and against everything that told him this night would be impossible.

The cold seeped into his bones, but it wasn't the storm that made him shiver. It was the fear that tugged at the edges of his mind. A fear he could not name. He wasn't just fighting the wind. He was fighting against the unknown, against the helplessness that gnawed at him, against the uncertainty of becoming a father at such an early age. Was he ready? Was he enough? The weight of the question pressed down on him with every step, making the miles feel longer and the wind sharper.

Every gust of wind grew fiercer, as though nature itself were challenging him. Yet my father did not falter. There was something in his steps, something in the way he moved through the storm, which spoke of a deep, quiet determination. It was his love for my mother that pushed him forward. It was the thought of me, waiting to be born in the chaos, which gave him strength. Every time he thought of turning back, the thought of her, so young and alone, kept him going.

The storms rage felt personal, as if it were testing him, but he was determined to pass. The weight of his mission pressed on him with every step, and as the wind howled, he thought about the world he was about to bring me into. Was it a world worth fighting for? A world full of storms, literal and metaphorical, where nothing seemed guaranteed? His mind raced, but he could not afford to lose focus. Every second counted. He had to reach my mother. The storm roared like a living thing, clawing at him, trying to turn him back. But my father's journey was not one of hope; it was a march of necessity. The future had already begun, and the battle to ensure it would not be defined by nature's whims had already begun. Love, he had learned, was not about comfort or ease it was a battle. A fight. A decision to face the storm rather than retreat from it. As he struggled against the storm, the air itself seemed to conspire against him. The storm was not simply nature's fury it was an omen, a sign of the tumultuous road ahead.

The world he was fighting to bring me into would be one of survival, a battleground where even love would face the winds of indifference.

It wasn't until the first light of dawn broke through the clouds, lighting the sky in hues of violet and pink, that my father's journey reached its end. He arrived at the hospital, exhausted but triumphant. His body ached from the cold, from the weight of the journey, but his resolve remained unbroken. The storm had tested him, but it could not defeat him. He had faced it head-on, and now, like the storm itself, he stood ready to face whatever came next. I was born just as the storm began to lose its ferocity. My first cry joined the diminishing roar of the wind in the early hours of January 16th, a small, fragile sound in the chaos that surrounded it. I like to think my first breath carried the same strength and determination as my father's steps. A cry that, even in its fragility, announced the arrival of a new beginning in a world that resisted change. My life, from the very start, would be a fight. But like my father, I would endure, because survival wasn't about avoiding the storm, but about facing it head-on.

Chapter 2

Early Wanderings

Our early life played out like a nomadic tale, the constant shuffle of cardboard boxes and the metallic jingle of new keys becoming our family's soundtrack. Every time we moved, something changed new smells, new rooms, unfamiliar places where we had to learn how to live again. The old houses always felt strange, like they didn't belong to us. The wood on the floor creaked, and the walls whispered secrets. Sometimes, I would lie awake in the dead of night, listening to the sounds of things that weren't there anymore the faint hum of old radiators, the wind rattling the windows like it was trying to get in. Six houses before I turned five each place had its own way of feeling, and none of them ever felt like home.

But in 1972, everything changed. The sharp antiseptic smell of hospital corridors stayed with me for months cold, like a place where people were too sick to leave. My father was in bed a lot, and he didn't look like himself. His hands were swollen, like balloons, and his body seemed smaller, weaker, as though his strength had been drained away. He didn't get up to play with me anymore. I missed the man who was once full of energy, the one who would lift me high into the air and tell me I could fly. Now, he was just a shadow of himself, unable to be the father I had known. His eyes were always distant, and his silence pressed down on the room, heavy and thick. The man I had once counted on had disappeared, and I didn't know if he would ever come back.

But even more than the absence of my father, it was the cruelty of my mother that I began to feel. I had no words for it then, but now I understand it clearly: she was cold, distant, and capable of violence. She would retreat into herself, a black hole of anger and bitterness that consumed everything around her. I remember how her face would twist when things didn't go her way eyes sharp, lips pulled back in a sneer. She would punish us, not just for our mistakes, but for existing, as if our very presence made her life harder. It wasn't just physical pain; it was the way her anger felt, like it could burn right through you. "Her punishments were swift and violent her hand hitting, her words cutting deep, and her ability to hold a grudge was nothing short of Olympic level."

I started to retreat, too. I would try to avoid her gaze, but she would always find me, her anger like a storm waiting to break. There was no way to stop it, no way to hide from it. It was always there, just beneath the surface, and I never knew when it would explode. It felt like walking through a house made of glass one wrong move and everything would shatter.

When my father recovered, he was no better. He wasn't the man I remembered. He didn't comfort me the way he used to, didn't reassure me that everything would be okay. Instead, his silence seemed to stretch between us like a chasm, growing wider with each passing day. I couldn't understand why he had stopped fighting. His illness had broken him, but worse, it had turned him into someone I feared. He was no longer the protector I had once known. Now, he was as broken as I felt. He couldn't protect us. He didn't know how to, or he didn't want to. That thought haunted me the idea that he had given up, that we were on our own in a world that felt more like a battlefield than a home. My mother, on the other hand, was unpredictable. Sometimes she would snap for no reason at all, her anger igniting over the smallest things. A misplaced toy. A forgotten chore. The pressure of living with her cruelty, and my father's inability to shield us from it, built up inside me.

But I didn't know where to put it. So, I buried it deep, hidden away in the darkest corners of my mind, hoping that if.

I didn't think about it, it would go away. But it didn't.
We stayed in a place called Finsbury Park in London. I have only small memories here and most of them racist. My dad had a way of calling everybody a chocolate biscuit. I didn't know what he meant really. I was on the bus with my dad one day and a big, huge Black man got on the bus. I said look dad a chocolate biscuit you should have seen my dad's face he was frightened. I was just repeating what he always said. The big man laughed and ruffled my curly ginger hair and said to me look a ginger nut, he laughed so did I. My dad was a bit quiet, but he learned a lesson. I can remember a day though when I got lost, I had been playing in the park out the front I can remember trying to go home I must have left the park on the wrong entrance. I can remember being lost and wandering forever looking for the house. But I couldn't see it, there was a shop, I went in there and stood. The shopkeeper noticed me and knew who I was I think my impressive red curly hair must have stood out. He gave me some chocolate sat me down. He must have sent for ma parents because mum arrived soon. She was angry she did not know I was missing till her door had

been locked. She kept hitting me saying that I had made her look like a cunt. We moved from there to Glasgow shortly after. Dad could never keep a job, so we moved.

We stayed in a tenement building in the centre of Glasgow I remember it well. There's a reason, and the reason is both funny and not funny. Tenement buildings didn't have inhouse toilets. Instead, there was a toilet on the in-between landings, shared by two families. This is where I was potty trained, where I learned to go myself.

Now, and this was always the case, some bastard kept stealing the light bulb. They took it for their own flat, or maybe they just enjoyed watching us stumble about in the dark. Or, and this is possible, I just couldn't reach the switch. Either way, it was pitch black in there.

The toilet paper was the daily newspaper, cut into squares, strung up with a bit of string and a nail. Nothing like the feel of yesterday's headlines on your backside. I didn't know any better, so I went when I needed to. It's amazing what you can learn to do in the dark like origami with the Daily Record.

Now, there was a pet store downstairs, and I used to spend all my time there, helping the man with the animals. He was a kindly old fella who didn't seem to mind a wee lad underfoot. He shows me the rabbits, the budgies, and the parrots. One of the parrots was called Jack and oh boy, could he swear.

In not talking a mild hello or pretty bird. Jack had a mouth on him that would make a docker blush. The old man swore it wasn't him that taught the parrot those words. Must've been the customers, he would say, his face an innocent mask. Id stand there, eyes wide, listening to a parrot rattle off a string of profanities that I knew I'd get a clout for repeating. The bird had better comic timing than most of the grown-ups I knew. Upstairs from us were two ladies who shared a flat they used to watch me a lot. I can't remember their names, but I heard my mum way once what they did for work. And that would make the parrot blush.

Chapter 3

School Daze

I started school when I was four, in Easterhouse, Glasgow. The other kids didn't know me, and I didn't know them probably because I spent most of my time perfecting the art of becoming invisible. Turns out, if you avoid eye contact long enough, people really do stop seeing you. I remember standing alone in the playground, watching them play from the sidelines. They were loud, full of life, and I didn't always understand what they were doing. I didn't want to fight, but sometimes they would push me, and then I would push back. I didn't know how to make them stop without fighting. It made me feel scared and small, and I didn't know how to talk to them. It was easier to be alone, even then.

I can't remember my mother or father ever taking me to school. I don't think it was the done thing back then. There was no hand to hold as I crossed the road, no goodbye wave from the school gate. You just showed up, like you had always been there, as if you had sprouted from the pavement overnight. I'd walk through the gates on my own, shoes scuffing against the tarmac, the weight of my satchel pulling on my shoulder. I'd watch the other kids arriving some with their parents, others like me, drifting in unnoticed. It felt like I'd been dropped into someone else's story, a background character with no lines.

Everything about school was big the building, the noise, the playground. I was so small, and the world loomed over me, all brick and sky. I learned early on how to blend in, to become part of the scenery. If I stood by the fence, under the tree, and kept my head down, I could disappear. The teachers didn't notice me unless I made a noise, and the kids only noticed me when they wanted someone to push. I took to walking around the edges of the playground, my fingers brushing against the rough stone walls, pretending I was on a journey somewhere far away. Anywhere but there.

There are things I don't remember. Faces, names, even voices. It's like looking through a fogged-up window- shapes and shadows, but nothing clear. I know I was there because I have the school photo somewhere, the one where I'm standing on the end of the row, half cut off by the edge of the picture. I was the kid you'd miss if you blinked. It's not the details that have stayed with me but the feeling.

That cold twist in my stomach, the way my skin prickled when someone got too close, the ache of loneliness that sat in my chest like a stone. I didn't know then that it was loneliness. I thought it was normal, the way everyone felt. The funny thing is, looking back, I preferred it that way. There's a comfort in being invisible. No expectations, no disappointments. I could watch the world from a safe distance, keeping my secrets to myself. It wasn't much, but it was mine. And when you don't have much else, you hold on to what you've got.

Chapter 4

If I can't have you, no one will.

Her hands were iron. Cold. Unyielding. Her calloused fingers dug into the nape of my neck, not with anger but with something darker something primal. The kind of force that didn't just want to hurt but to erase. It wasn't even the bath. It was the kitchen sink, the one where dishes were scrubbed raw and potatoes were peeled down to their bones. The water sloshed over the rim, soaking the linoleum, turning the faded floral patterns into wet, distorted flowers drowning under glass. The whole room reeked of old soap and blood, the copper tang of it biting the back of my throat. She pushed us both under. My sister and I, side by side, crammed into the sink, our heads forced beneath the water. Her hair brushed against my cheek, a cold, silken thread that only made the water feel tighter around us. We were tangled together, two bodies compressed into porcelain, our limbs knotted and useless. I could feel her shivering, her small body pressed against mine, our desperate breaths mingling in the water as

bubbles escaped from our mouths. The world became a muffled roar, sounds warping and twisting like they couldn't quite find us. I opened my
mouth to scream, and the water flooded in, sharp and icy. The bubbles floated up, delicate and mocking, fragile pieces of us rising to the surface and bursting into nothing. My lungs seized, a red-hot pain spreading out from my ribs, a scream turned inward.

Those bubbles still haunt me. They pop in my nightmares, in those tight spaces where air seems thinner, where walls close in and the world narrows to a pinpoint. The burn in my chest comes back, searing, and relentless, like a brand pressed against my ribs. It happens when I'm anxious, when I'm asleep, when There's no corner left to hide in.

Her face was right there, turned towards me. Her eyes were open, wide, and glassy, a pale blue clouded by fear. Her lips moved under the water, but no sound came. She was close enough to touch, but my arms wouldn't move, heavy and waterlogged. I could feel the cold of her skin, the brush of her hair against my face, and yet she felt so far away. Blood bloomed. Red smoke swirling in the water. Her head had hit the tap, the sharp crack of it reverberating through my bones. The water turned pink, a pastel horror. I tasted copper, sharp and metallic, the kind of taste that fills your mouth when you bite your tongue to keep from crying out. I couldn't spit it out. Couldn't scream. My mouth was full of water, my breath a razor slicing through my chest.

Above it all, I heard her. My mother. Her voice was a jagged thing, a blade dragged across stone.

"If I can't have you, no one will!"

Her words clung to the air, each one a stone strapped to our ankles, pulling us further under. Her hands pressed down, the lip of the sink biting into our scalps. Every time we fought, she shoved harder, until my vision narrowed to the sloshing, blood-tinged water and the dim kitchen light fractured through the soapy surface.

I felt myself shrinking. We both did. We were not children anymore. We were less than that. Smaller than a whisper, smaller than a shadow. Just fragments, slivers of fear suspended in chilly water. The weight of her anger was an avalanche, burying us alive, not in snow but in water and blood and a chill that gnawed its way to our bones.

Some quiet part of me, tucked away in the marrow of my bones, whispered that this was it. The thought was almost peaceful, a lullaby sung by the dark. It would be easier to let go, to sink into the cold, to let it fill every hollow space inside me. It would be quiet there. No more screams. No more hands dragging us under. No more weight.

And then the world exploded.
The door didn't just open it detonated. The frame shuddered, plaster crumbling, the whole room jolting. My dad was there, his voice a roar that rattled the tiles. His rage filled the room, thick and tangible, a new force pushing against the water.

"What the fuck are you doing, you crazy bitch?"

There was a blur a flash of flesh and fury. A sound like wet meat slapped against stone. My mothers grip slipped, her hands finally breaking away. Her head snapped back, a bloom of red at her mouth, and then she was on the floor. The thud of her body against the linoleum was a hollow sound, like something breaking deep inside the earth. The water calmed, ripples fading to a stillness that felt wrong, like the silence after a storm. My sister and I sat there, soaked and shivering, our chests heaving, skin pale and clammy. I still tasted blood, the phantom sting of it on my tongue. The cold had burrowed deep into my bones, a frost that would never fully thaw.

My dad stood over her, his fists still clenched, breathing in ragged, heaving gasps. His eyes were wild, an animal at the edge of a precipice. I'd never seen him hit her before.

Relief, fear, and confusion tangled together, a knot of barbed wire in my chest. But those hands, the ones that had pressed us under were gone. And I could breathe.

The air tasted sharp, laced with the echoes of screams and the raw, lingering scent of violence. My sister's wide eyes met mine, and in that look, I saw it something fractured, something vital lost. We were just kids, but that day, our childhood went under with us and never came back up. I wish I could say it was the last time. It was not. The bath became a battlefield, every brush with water a skirmish where we had to fight for air. To this day, water wraps itself around my fear, pulling it tight. I can swim. I can go under. But only on my terms. The moment I feel a hand on me, the panic hits like a fist to the gut. It's a fear that lives just beneath my skin, a second shadow, always waiting to drag me under.

Funny. My favourite things are to do with water. I trained myself to feel the fear and push forward anyway. That is what she taught me, I suppose. To survive. To learn how to hold my breath, how to float, how to swim back to the surface no matter how deep I sank. It was her way of giving me a gift, a twisted lesson in resilience. Well, lesson learned.

I did not understand why it happened. What had I done to make her so angry? I felt like I was drowning in questions, each one another hand pulling me down. When my dad pulled us from the water, I felt a wash of relief, but it was only a surface thing. Underneath, the cold had already taken root.

And now, looking back, I can almost laugh. The dark kind, the bitter kind, the kind that tastes like blood in your mouth. Like a joke with teeth. How do you teach kids to hold their breath? You don't. You just keep them under until they stop struggling. Until they get the point. It's a joke; I'll never say it aloud. But it lives there, a chuckle in the back of my mind. A razor-edged coping mechanism honed sharp over years of learning how to breathe through the water, through the fear, through the weight of hands that always wanted us under.

And yet, here we are. Still breathing. Still here. And maybe That's the real joke the punchline to a story no one ever asked to hear. We survived. We learned how to swim, and we've been swimming ever since.

Chapter 5

They Broke the Kids' Code

The park was the one place I could forget all the terrible things. The swings felt like flying, and the roundabout spun so fast it made my stomach turn. For a little while, I could pretend that nothing else mattered, that I was safe there. The rusted chains of the swings creaked in rhythm, a squeaky metronome marking the beats of my escape. The cold metal bit into my hands, but I didn't mind it was real, solid, a tether to something that wasnt fear.

My sister and I had a system, a kind of kids' code. She was my lookout, my trusty lieutenant. She'd sit up on the veranda, legs swinging through the rails, her high-pitched voice carrying across the concrete playground. 'Bugger off, this is our park!' she'd shout, and Id back her up, my scrawny frame full of righteous fury. She had a gift for insults, sharp and quick, delivered with all the bravado of a pint-sized general. It was us against the world, or at least against the boys who thought they could take our place. But when they didn't listen, when they stood their ground, something hot and twisted boiled up inside me. I didn't have the words, so I did the only thing of which I could think. I yanked my pants down and mooned them. A bare-arsed act of rebellion. My sister joined in, a double-barrelled assault of childish defiance. It should have been funny, but even then, I knew it was more than that. It was a warning. 'Stay away or else.'

We were just kids, five and four years old. It was silly, harmless fun the kind only kids understand. But one of the sneaky wee shites broke the code. He slithered off without us noticing, climbed the stairs, and told our mother what we'd done. And then everything changed.

When she came, it was like a storm breaking over us. She was thunder and lightning, sharp and sudden. I barely saw her coming before the slap hit me, a crack that echoed off the walls. My head snapped sideways, and for a second, everything was white noise and ringing.

She threw me against the wall, her hands still trembling with the force of her rage. I was a rag doll, all soft limbs, and wide eyes, too young to understand but old enough to know I was in trouble. My sister was crying too, her voice a thin wail that mixed with the distant sounds of the playground the swing chains still creaking, oblivious. But it wasn't just the slap, or the push, or the way her face turned red and twisted. It was the words. She called us things terrible, shameful things. She said we were like paedophiles, as if we'd done something dirty and wrong. I didn't even know what that meant back then. We were just kids, playing a game, but she turned it into something else, something ugly. She made it feel like a stain that wouldn't wash off. I could feel the dirt of it sinking into my skin, a grime that only got thicker the more I tried to understand. I wanted to comfort my sister, to be the big brother, the brave one. But I couldn't. I couldn't even comfort myself. Something inside me had busted, like a clockwork toy wound too tight until the springs snapped. The kids' code was broken, and nothing felt safe anymore.

Later, when the sting had faded but the hurt remained, we sat on the veranda together. My sisters' eyes were red rimmed, and I could see the question there why? Why had we been punished for protecting our place? I didn't have an answer, so I told her a story instead. A made-up tale about secret agents and hidden treasure, our park transformed into a jungle, the boys into villains with evil plans. She giggled, and for a moment, it almost felt okay.

But in the back of my mind, the storm still lingered, a promise of more to come. I learned that day that storms don't just pass they stay with you, waiting for the next chance to break.

Chapter 6

A Night in the Park

The park was never the same after the sun set. In the daylight, it was a place of games, of children running and laughing, their shouts filling the air. But as dusk descended, the park shifted into something darker. The shadows stretched longer, curling around the edges of the playground equipment like they were hiding secrets. The once sparkling swings now creaked in the wind, their chains rattling in a way that didn't feel right like they were trying to call someone.

I didn't usually go out at night, but I had to get the cigarettes for Mum. She always sent me to the corner shop, and the walk there took me right through the park. Most of the time, I would rush through, trying not to look at the darker corners where I knew the older kids hung out. But tonight, something felt different.

The streetlights cast sickly yellow glows over the concrete paths, flickering every few seconds like they were struggling to stay on. The trees, once full of life, now stood like sentinels bare and foreboding. It felt like the air was heavier, thick with the sense of something about to happen. As I cut through the park, I tried not to look at the bench where the old men sat, talking in whispers I couldn't understand. I wasn't meant to be here after dark, but I had no choice. That's when I saw them. A figure, dark against the dim lights, leaning over another. The first thing I noticed was the glint of metal. At first, I thought it was some sort of prank, someone messing around with a tool, but then the air was pierced by the sound an awful thud, followed by a sickening crack. The man in the shadows swung what looked like an axe again, this time hitting the other in the back, right between the shoulder blades. The man on the ground didn't scream. He just crumpled, his body folding in on itself like a rag doll. The sound of the impact echoed through the empty park, reverberating off the swings, the slides, the trees. My heart skipped a beat, my legs frozen to the spot. I wanted to run, but my feet wouldn't move. I didn't know if it was the shock of seeing something so... wrong, or if it was the fear of being seen, but I couldn't tear my eyes away. The man with the axe stepped back, his figure shadowed by the night, as if he were part of the dark itself.

He glanced around, his eyes scanning, but he didn't seem to see me. The other man on the ground lay still, his face turned toward the ground in the dirt, blood pooling around him in small, dark circles. I didn't know what to do. I was just a kid, too young for this, too small to even understand the whole of it. I couldn't think straight. My mind was racing, but my body felt like it was made of stone. The park, once a place of escape, now felt like a cage, trapping me in a nightmare I couldn't wake up from. And then, as quickly as it had started, the man with the axe turned and disappeared into the darkness. The sound of his boots on the gravel faded as he walked away, leaving nothing behind but the blood-stained ground and the lingering scent of something that smelled like death.

I didn't run. I didn't scream. I just stood there, frozen, watching the park transform before my eyes. The swings creaked. The trees swayed in the wind. The darkness deepened. And I realised, as I stared at the lifeless body on the ground, that this was the world into which I was growing. A world where the dark corners of the park weren't just for playing, but for something much, much worse.

I didn't look back as I turned and walked toward the shop. I didn't want to see any more. I just wanted to get the cigarettes and go home. But even as I walked, the image of the man's crumpled body and the sound of that axe still echoed in my mind. I couldn't shake it. It was something I'd never be able to forget, no matter how hard I tried. As I look back it was the start of the ice cream wars, I can't be positive, but it suddenly became a time when you were scared to go to the ice cream van. For those that don't know ice cream vans were being used by organised crime guys in the east of Glasgow. Places like Easterhouse were rife from the start of the seventies till the mid-1980s. I'd seen blue like oil thrown on the window of an ice cream van with the other van then overtaking the run. It seemed to have been a serious business.

Chapter 7

My Grand Fathers Garden

My grandfather, the council gardener, left his mark on our town in many ways. His expertise shone through in the welcome garden, where he meticulously arranged flowers to spell out our town's name. It wasn't just a garden it was a tribute to the land he loved, a quiet act of pride. The garden stood as a testament to his care, a place where nature and his careful hands intertwined in perfect harmony. But it was his kitchen windowsill that held my personal favourite flourishing tomato plant that became my first lesson in patience and nurturing.

"Can I try one now, Granddad?" I'd ask, my small hands itching to pluck the ripening tomatoes from their vines. The scent of the garden, earthy and fresh, seemed to wrap around me, filling the air with the promise of growth and renewal. I stood at his side, wide-eyed with anticipation, watching the ripening fruits hanging heavy in the sun. "Not yet, wee man," he'd say with a warm smile, his eyes crinkling at the corners like the edges of worn pages. "Nature has its own time. Strong roots make strong flowers."

His voice was like a gentle wind, steady and reassuring. I learned then that good things didn't come easily, and that waiting was a lesson. His hands rough with age and years of demanding work moved gracefully over the plants, coaxing them into life with a touch that was both firm and tender. He taught me that patience was a skill, not just a waiting game. "The earth rewards care," he would say, and I felt it in every plant he nurtured, every garden he tended. His touch, soft yet purposeful, showed me that time and care could yield something beautiful.

But the truth is, I never got to eat that tomato. It sat on the kitchen windowsill, ripening under the warm Scottish sun, a tiny promise of sweetness I never tasted. Life moved on, as it does, and the tomato, like so many other things, slipped away. I often think of it the missed chance, the quiet lesson in longing it left behind. Even in the greenhouse, where rows of tomatoes hung heavy on their vines, I never plucked one for myself. The anticipation, the hope of it, remained just that a hope, suspended in time. It wasn't until much later in life that I finally ate a tomato straight off the vine. I remember the moment vividly, the way the skin gave way under my teeth, the burst of flavour, and the way the scent filled the air a smell so rich, so earthy, it was like stepping back into my grandfather's garden. It was as if the years folded in on themselves, and I was a boy again, standing by his side, waiting for that simple, perfect taste.

Since then, I've tried growing tomatoes myself. Some years are better than others, and I'll try again this year, hoping to capture a piece of that past. Supermarket tomatoes, with their polished skins and hollow scent, don't compare. They lack the fragrance that lingers in the greenhouse air the smell that, for me, is transcendent. You can get latched onto a smell, I suppose. For me, it's the smell of tomatoes, the scent of a memory, and a promise of something just out of reach.

Hanging above the overhang of the front door, a miner's lamp swayed gently in the breeze. Its glass was clouded with age, but it still held the echoes of its past. My grandfather used to tell me stories from the coal mines, his voice low and steady as if the words were meant to stay between us. He would point out where the old miners' raws had been, where men like him had once walked home, coal dust lining the creases of their skin.

He missed the camaraderie of the mines, the sense of purpose that demanding work gave. "Hard work, but someone had to do it," he would say. "Might as well have been me." His words carried no bitterness, only a quiet pride. There was a fellowship in the mines, he said, a bond forged in the dark and the dust that stayed with him long after he left. The lamp, a relic of those days, seemed to hold a soft glow even when unlit, a reminder of where he had been and the stories that would live on through him.

The garden was a metaphor, a life lesson. Each motion was deliberate and full of purpose, like the lessons he would impart to me. He was teaching me not only how to care for a garden but also how to care for life itself.

I followed him as he worked, tracing every move of his hands as they pruned, watered, and shaped the land. We spent hours together in the garden. My small hands would mimic his movements as best as I could. He taught me how to dig how to loosen the soil, to turn it over so it could breathe. "You have to be gentle with it," he'd say, patting the soil after he had turned it, "and the garden will give you what you need."

Watching him move in the earth was like watching an artist at work, his hands shaping life from soil, coaxing it into being. I had no idea then how much those lessons would stay with me, shaping how I approached not just gardens, but everything in life.

It was with my grandfather and uncles that I first learned what it meant to be part of a family. Time was shared not through grand gestures but in simple moments, in the quiet way we sat together after a long day of work. The world outside may have felt chaotic, but here, in the garden and the kitchen, there was an undeniable sense of stability. And then there was my father.

Different here than at home. He laughed and joked with my uncles, his usual tension slipping away under the warmth of my grandfather's roof. It was as if, here in this space, he could be himself again. More alive, more present his laughter filled the air, light and free, ringing out like a song. I wondered, even then, why he could be so different here. Why, when we were home, did he seem so distant, so burdened by invisible weight? At my grandfather's house, he shed his burdens, even if only for a little while. I wanted to hold onto that laughter, to make it stay, but it always felt fleeting like something too fragile to keep. That garden, that kitchen, those moments they were the roots that kept me grounded, the vines that stretched through my life, always leading me back to that sense of home.

Chapter 8

Moving Back to My Hometown

The family moved back to Hamilton when I was around six. We settled in an area of town that had been dubbed "Wine Valley." It was a strange name for a place, but to me, it was home. There was my house, next door was my uncles, and just around the corner lived my dad's other brother. It was good to be close to my cousins again. We didn't go to the same school, but we played together every evening. The woods and trees surrounding our houses became our playground, a place where imagination could run wild, and the world outside seemed distant. It felt like the beginning of a new chapter, a chance for stability family reunited.

There was a ravine behind my house, and I would often wander down there, my bow and arrow in hand, a gift from my uncle Rennie. He had made them for me, carving the wood with care, the arrow fletched with feathers that tickled my fingers as I held it. I felt strong with my bow, as if I could be the hero of a story, taking on whatever dangers the woods threw at me. I would sneak past the boundary of the yard, pretending to be a mighty warrior hunting in the wild.

The air smelled of damp earth and the sweet scent of fallen leaves, and for a moment, I felt invincible like I could conquer anything.

One day, while trying to reach the arrow that had gotten stuck up a tree, I stood on the slick, muddy ground beneath. My feet slipped, and the next thing I knew, I was falling. The shock of the icy water when I hit it was immediate. I remember the coldness seeping through my t-shirt, the fabric clinging to me as I sank deeper into the ravine. Panic surged in my chest, my heart racing as my body struggled against the water. I felt the pull of the current as it dragged me down, my breath coming in sharp gasps. My collar t-shirt caught on a low-hanging branch behind me, pulling me back, and my face was half-submerged in the dark water. My hands reached out, grasping for anything to hold onto, but there was nothing.

I screamed, the water rushing into my mouth, choking me, and my cries were muffled by the gurgling of the stream. I thought I was going to drown, and the thought of it sent terror through me. My limbs were too heavy, my body too small against the unforgiving force of the water. And then, as if from nowhere, I heard a voice a deep, commanding voice, familiar but not. It was my grandfather's sister's son, a man I barely knew but who was family, nonetheless. He had been walking past, and he heard my cries. His large hands reached down, strong fingers wrapping around my arms, pulling me with an urgency I'd never felt before. His hands were warm, like an anchor in the sea of panic. The relief that washed over me when he lifted me out of the water was more than I could manage. I remember clinging to him; my tiny arms wrapped around his neck as he held me close. His arms were strong, and for the first time in what felt like forever, I felt safe.

He didn't say much, just whispered assurances that I was going to be okay. But his presence, his steady hands, made everything feel calm again. It was like a light in the dark, something I hadn't realised I was craving. As he carried me back to my parents, I felt like I was being rescued from something much deeper than just the ravine. In his embrace, the protection Id longed for, the promise of safety. For a moment, nothing else mattered. But safety, it seemed, was short-lived. I now realise that I have family of my own, and I can understand how parents can get scared and angry when things like this happen. But what I learned that day was that anger could sometimes cloud judgement, leading a parent to cross lines they should never approach. After that, my father's anger didn't just frighten me it scarred me. When he saw me, wet and trembling in my rescuer's arms, it wasn't relief that showed in his eyes, but something darker. He took a stick a broken branch, jagged with a nail sticking out and struck me across the head. The pain was instant, sharp, and overwhelming. I remember the crack of the wood against my skull, the sting of it, the weight of it as it sent me to the ground. My vision blurred, and for a moment, I didn't understand what had happened. The world tilted sideways, and the confusion overwhelmed me. How could the man who had just carried me to safety now be the one to hurt me? I didn't even have time to process it before my dad's two sisters, who had been at my uncles' house, burst into the room. They heard the shouting, the violence, and my cries. They rushed in, their voices filled with panic and anger as they took me in their arms, away from the chaos. One of them immediately took me to my grandparents' house, while the other made sure to get a doctor to look at my head.

I stayed with my grandparents for a couple of nights. The house was different a calm, a respite from the storm of my own home. But the uncertainty lingered. My parents came to visit, and their faces were strained with anger. My auntie had already told my mother and father that they had reported them to the "cruelty man," a social worker who could take children away if things were bad enough. That's when I realised how serious things were.

The room was bare walls the colour of porridge, a single chair, and a desk that had seen better days. I could almost hear my parents breathing through the door, their presence as solid as if they were standing right behind me. The man crouched down to my level, his knees cracking with the effort. He had a kind face, the sort that might belong to a character in a storybook the ones who always helped lost children find their way home. The irony of it wasn't lost on me.

"So, tell me what happened," he asked, his voice soft. "I fell on the stick," I said, just like my dad had taught me. I delivered the line like a well-rehearsed actor, hitting my mark.

"Are you scared of your dad?"

I shook my head, forcing a smile. "No, I love my dad." Exactly like he had told me to say. It felt like pulling a mask over my face, the kind that only fools strangers. When the man turned away and went back into the other room, I allowed myself a sliver of hope. Things would change. He would see through it all and make my dad kinder. But hope, like everything else, had a way of slipping through my fingers.

The door closed behind him, and I knew. Whatever Id imagined might happen, it wasn't that. Not even close.

Chapter 9

Another Day to my Ravine

Another day at the ravine I never did learn a lesson. The ravine had always been my kingdom. I wasn't just a kid playing in the mud; I was a swashbuckling hero, a daring adventurer, just like the characters in the old pirate movies I used to watch. I imagined myself swinging from tree to tree, leaping from one branch to the next, like I was crossing from sail to sail on a ship in the middle of a storm. In my mind's eye, I was Jack Hawkins brave and unstoppable, navigating through uncharted waters. The wind in my hair, the leaves rustling beneath my feet, every leap felt like a new victory.

One day, with the sun high above and my imagination running wild, I spotted the perfect tree. Its branches hung low, strong enough to hold my weight, and I felt the excitement stir in my chest. I climbed up with ease, using the thick trunk as my anchor before swinging out into the air. I felt free, weightless, as if I were flying, the ground far below me.

In my mind, I was already leaping across the deck of a pirate ship, but my hands weren't quite as sure as my imagination. My left hand, slick with sweat, slipped from the branch just as I swung toward the next one. I didn't even have time to react. The next thing I knew, my body was hurtling toward the ground, and I landed with a sharp, jarring pain.

My foot slipped on the muddy ground, but it wasn't the mud that caught me. It was the old fence post sticking up from the earth, jagged and waiting. The force of my fall impaled me, the sharp wood driving straight into my side. I gasped, a sharp pain shooting through me as the world spun for a moment. For a few seconds, I thought I might pass out, but the pain snapped me back into the moment. My mind raced. God, I thought I was so clever, so invincible. There I was, trying to live out my swashbuckling fantasy, and I ended up skewered on a fence post like a fool. My whole body felt heavy, like I was drowning in my own stupidity. I'd been so focused on the leap, so caught up in the adventure, that I hadn't even considered the risk.

But then, something strange happened. As I stood there, with the post stuck inside me, all I could do was laugh. It wasn't a loud, triumphant laugh, but a quiet chuckle, a realisation that this was just one of those things. One of those dumb, brave, and completely unnecessary adventures that my imagination always got me into. It was a reminder that sometimes, no matter how clever we think we are, life has a way of knocking us back down, and no amount of fantasy can protect you from the consequences of your own recklessness.

I remember pulling myself off the fence post, the pain sharp and real, but the experience somehow funny in retrospect. My imagination had gotten me into trouble once again, but it had also given me a story something to smile about years later. It's funny how those memories, the ones that seemed so intense and painful at the time, can turn into little moments of joy as we grow older.

I always had a way of imagining myself as something bigger than I was, something braver, something untouchable. And, looking back, I realise that that was the magic of it all getting caught up in the fantasy, even if it sometimes led to a fence post through your side. I can remember that year on bonfires night what a display we got. They set a house on fire all the families were out watching the blaze. Police and the fire brigade came to put out the flames. It was the best bonfire I had ever seen the house was empty the family had been evicted their stuff was still in the house and it all burned down. Partly because the locals wouldn't let the police and fire brigade into the street. There were stones thrown and names called. First time I had a potato cooked in a fire. It was burnie on my hands I didn't understand the danger then. I do now the firefighters went into the house and risked their lives for no one.

Chapter 10

Fists Clenched at My Side

A few months later we were walking home as a family, the quiet weight of the moment hanging around us. We had just been to the doctors, and it felt strange for all of us to be out together. These moments were rare, where the tension at home seemed to disappear, replaced by the fleeting normalcy of simply walking side by side. But even in that strange calm, there was always an undercurrent of unease, something pulling at the edges of the peace.

The path we took was familiar, but the feeling that clung to the air was different. The smell of damp earth, mingled with the faint scent of old cigarettes from the corner shop, made everything feel heavier than it should have. As we neared my grandfather's house, I felt that tight knot in my stomach again. The house stood like a landmark in my childhood, full of memories but I had learned not to get too close.

We had to be quick. We couldn't let my grandparents see us not because I didn't want to, but because it was better that way. There was always something about being seen by them that felt too much to bear too complicated, too revealing. It was as if walking past their house meant exposing the parts of us that we weren't allowed to talk about. I was used to silence, to hiding things, but even in my young mind, I understood that some things could never be fully concealed.

My parents often hid things from my grandparents. It wasn't because they didn't love us, I knew that much, but because there were things they didn't want anyone to see. Every visit to my grandparents was filled with unspoken rules, things we couldn't say, things about which we couldn't talk. My mother used to take us up to see them once a week, but before we went in, we were always told the same thing: Don't say anything about your dad. Don't talk about what you had to eat. Don't mention anything that might make us look bad.

It was like we were expected to keep up a facade, to pretend that everything was perfect when it never was. The fear of saying something wrong, something that would get us into trouble with our parents, made every visit feel suffocating. When we were inside, we would sit in the living room, trying to appear calm, but always terrified of saying something we shouldn't. I would look around at my siblings, hoping they wouldn't say something that would break the rules, but we all knew our mouths were closed, our eyes lowered, and silence was the safest choice. The visits always ended the same way. My grandparents, despite everything, always gave us pocket money before we left. I remember the warmth in their hands as they passed the coins to us, the love in their eyes, the way they wanted to make sure we knew we were cared for. But without fail, every time, my mother would take the money from us. I don't know why, but it was like a part of the ritual. She would take the money and put it in her purse, and we would be left feeling empty, like something that was meant to be ours was taken from us again.

It wasn't because my grandparents didn't love us it was because my parents had made us part of a game we didn't fully understand, a game where we were the pawns. The secrecy, the lies, the manipulation everything felt so heavy, like the air itself was thick with things unsaid. And as I walked past my grandfather's house that day, I couldn't shake the tension in the pit of my stomach.

I had grown used to the lies, to the things I wasn't allowed to say. But now, as I saw my grandfather's angry face through the window, I couldn't help but feel the years of that strained relationship crashing down on me. He was angry, but I knew it wasn't about what had happened that day. It was about everything that had been hidden from him, everything he hadn't known about us. I felt the weight of all the secrets we had kept, and it crushed me. I stepped forward, fists clenched tightly at my sides, trying to hold on to something anything that made sense. My heart was pounding, a quick rhythm in my chest, but I was tired of pretending. I will never forgive you for this! I shouted, my voice breaking through the air, raw with confusion and hurt. I was sticking up for my father, but I had also just broken something with my grandfather. I could see the shock in his eyes, the hurt that my words had caused him, and it was like everything had shattered in that moment. My grandfather had always called me Speug, a baby bird, fragile and needing care. He had held me as a child, swaddled in cloth, calling me his little bird, and in that moment, I wished more than anything to be that child again, safe in his arms, protected from the world. But I had hurt him with my words, and I could see the pain in his eyes, a pain that I could never take away.

I had been so focused on protecting my father, on standing up for him, that I hadn't stopped to think about the consequences of my actions. I wanted to be his Speug, but I had pushed my grandfather away, and I couldn't take back what I had said. I had hurt him when all I wanted was to be loved and understood.

But standing up for my father had always come first. It was an instinct I couldn't shake. Even if my father was wrong if he had made mistakes, I still felt this deep need to protect him, to shield him from the world's judgement. It's something I've carried with me my entire life. I've always had this urge to fight for the underdog, to speak for those who couldn't, even when they didn't deserve it. I had been so focused on protecting my father, on standing up for him, that I hadn't stopped to think about the consequences of my actions like an underdog in a fight who realises halfway through that he is actually just a dog."

It's a part of me, this unwavering need to make sure that the vulnerable aren't forgotten, even when the line between right and wrong blurs. Yet, in that moment, I realised something else. Sometimes standing up for someone doesn't mean you ignore their flaws. It doesn't mean you protect them from the consequences of their actions, no matter how much you love them. Sometimes, the hardest thing is knowing when to walk away and when to speak out not because it's easy, but because it's necessary for everyone's growth. It's something Ice had to learn over the year show to pick my battles. Some, I let go. Some, I'll never budge on. But I now know that the cost of always protecting others, of always standing by them even when they're wrong, can be more than you can afford. In the end, the silence that I had learned to live withstanding by while others spoke for me, speaking for others wasn't always the answer. Sometimes, the hardest thing is finding your voice, even when you know it might hurt.

Chapter 11

The Bull in the Field

One day, my dad decided to take us for a walk across the country fields. It was a beautiful, sunny day, the kind where the sky stretched endlessly above and the grass swayed gently in the breeze. The warmth of the sun on my neck felt good, though there was still a slight nip in the air. The gentle hum of nature surrounded us, birds chirping, the rustling of leaves but even during such tranquillity, I could feel something lurking beneath the surface. It was the kind of day where everything felt calm, almost idyllic. We walked as a family, the simplicity of it all grounding me in the moment. But that peace wouldn't last long.

As we walked along, we noticed a cow in the distance. At first, it seemed like just another peaceful part of the countryside. The animal grazed lazily, its silhouette framed by the bright green of the fields. But as we got closer, something didn't feel quite right. There was a stillness in the air, the kind you get when the world suddenly holds its breath. The birds had stopped singing, the wind seemed to hold still, and my dad seemed to tense up as he looked more closely at the animal.

I watched him, his brow furrowing, his body becoming rigid. He took a step back, eyes narrowing, as the truth of the situation dawned on him. What we had thought was a cow was no cow at all it was a bull, and it wasn't standing still anymore.

I could see the change in his demeanour immediately. His posture shifted, and that calm, steady voice of his that usually reassured us now carried an edge of urgency. Without warning, he turned and sprinted ahead, shouting for us to follow. Panic seeped into his voice quick, sharp, and unmistakable. This wasn't a passive animal anymore; this was something dangerous, and he knew it.

"Run!" my dad shouted, his voice urgent and loud, the command cutting through the air. His legs moved like lightning as he jumped over the fence and into the safety of the field on the other side. The thudding of my heart in my chest drowned out everything else for a moment. I looked back at my siblings, and panic surged through me, cold and sharp. We all scrambled, hearts pounding, adrenaline surging as the bull began to move toward us. It wasn't a slow, cautious pace; it was purposeful, its massive head lowering like it had already decided we were in its way. The sound of its hooves thundering against the earth grew louder, and my feet slip on the wet grass, my legs heavy with fear as I urged my siblings to move faster. I could hear the bulls' growls, the low rumble that sent chills down my spine. The weight of my fear pressed down on me, but the weight of my responsibility pressed harder. I couldn't just run I had to help them get over the fence, had to make sure they were safe.

I pushed myself harder, legs aching, trying to find my rhythm as the adrenaline coursed through me. The fence was ahead, but it felt impossibly far. The sounds of the bull's pursuit filled my ears, each step of its heavy charge reminding me of how little time we had. My dad's voice called out from the other side, shouting for us to hurry, urging us to move faster.

Finally, my hands reached the fence, the rough wood scraping against my fingers as I scrambled for a foothold. My feet slid in the mud, but I didn't care I pushed myself higher, heart racing in time with the panic in my chest. My siblings were already over, but I hesitated, looking back at the bull, its snorts and growls reverberating in the air like a final warning. I had to get over. I had to protect them. With a final burst of effort, I jumped, my hands gripping the top of the fence, and pulled myself over, landing hard on the other side. I looked back, still shaking, my breath coming in ragged gasps. There, standing in the field, was my dad, laughing. "Thought I was going to have to pull you all out of there!" he said, chuckling at the chaos of it all. His voice, always a source of reassurance, now seemed detached, light-heated, as if the moment had been nothing but a small adventure. He found it funny, as fathers do, laughing at the near disaster, making it sound like a joke, like it wasn't as close to life-threatening as it had been. But what he didn't know was that I was furious.

Not at him, not at my siblings but at myself. The anger bubbled up in my chest, thick and hot. I wasn't angry that my dad had run ahead he was protecting us, doing what any father would do. But the bitterness that settled inside me was born from the feeling that I had been left behind. In that moment, while I was scrambling to help my siblings, my dad had made it to safety first.

I couldn't shake the thought that in that moment, he had run ahead while I was left to scramble, to help everyone else before I got myself over. I had been focused on them on keeping them safe and had forgotten to keep myself safe too.

And then, in the space between my heart pounding and my hands trembling, I thought, You fucking coward. But it wasn't just anger. It was a feeling of being left out, of not being fast enough, not being the one in control when it mattered most. I wasn't proud of that thought. I knew my father had acted out of instinct, out of love, but that bitterness still lingered.

In later life, I understood why my father had acted the way he did. He saw the threat, recognized the danger, and did what he thought was right at the time. He was protecting us, running ahead to make sure he was safe, to ensure he could help us if we needed it. But still, the bitterness of that moment lingered in my chest, a reminder of that feeling of helplessness.

Now, I think back to that day and realise that if I were in that situation again, I would face the bull. Not out of bravery, but because I know what it means to protect your family. I don't think its bravery; it's simply a father's instinct.

Any father, any parent, would do the same to protect their children. You would stand in front of the danger, facing it down, just to make sure your kids are safe. It's not about fearlessness. It's about love. And love means doing what you can to make sure they survive, even if you're afraid.

Even if it weighs a tonne with murder in its eyes.

Chapter 12:

Treasure Island and Kidnapped

Content Warning: *References to poverty and childhood hardship.*

My grandfather the gardener gave me a gift that would change my life Treasure Island by Robert Louis Stevenson. It was a small, well-worn book, the kind that had passed through many hands before mine, its pages soft and frayed at the edges. But to me, it was a treasure greater than anything I could have imagined. In our home, where electricity was a luxury, we rarely enjoyed, I would lie in bed, the cold biting at my skin, reading by the faint glow of streetlights filtering through my window. The warmth of the Caribbean seas, the promise of adventure, and the vivid characters jumped from the pages, and for a brief time, the cold seemed less bitter, the hunger less gnawing. I was no longer trapped in the small, dark room with the sharp edges of my reality; I was Jim Hawkins, sailing toward treasure, fighting pirates, and experiencing a life of excitement that felt impossible in my own world.

"Fifteen men on the dead man's chest Yo-ho-ho, and a bottle of rum!" The words echoed in my mind as I turned each page, each verse a reminder of the wild adventure that awaited Jim Hawkins. In the world of pirates and treasure, there was always something bigger than hunger, bigger than the cramped space of my room. The book offered a world where everything could be magical, and the greatest challenge was survival, not the simple, gnawing ache of daily life.

By then, our family had grown to five children, and the meagre resources we had were stretched to breaking point. I remember the way my parents would encourage us to sleep after school, their gentle words masking the uncomfortable truth that there was no food for dinner. In those moments, the ache in my stomach was a constant companion, gnawing and unrelenting. But it was nothing compared to the solace I found in the pages of my book. Through its pages, I could feast on adventure. I could taste the salt of the sea and feel the thrill of the chase, as the characters in the book fought pirates and faced down dangers. I could escape to a world where hunger didn't exist, where the only thing that mattered was the quest for treasure.

Even when my body was hungry, my mind was full. The stories in Treasure Island gave me more than just a distraction they gave me a sense of hope. The world of Jim Hawkins and Long John Silver was solid, real in a way that my own world often wasn't. It was the one place where I could be more than just a child in a struggling family. I could be a part of something grand, a part of something bigger than myself, something important. "For a few hours each night, which was enough. Besides, Jim Hawkins never had to worry about who was going to give him a wallop for being late home. Lucky bastard."

Another book, Kidnapped, by the same author, also found its way into my hands, and it became just as important. In many ways, Kidnapped mirrored the same spirit of adventure, survival, and self-discovery that Treasure Island had awakened in me. The story of David Balfour, cast adrift in the world, seeking justice and grappling with survival on a journey filled with danger and intrigue, resonated deeply with me. Like David, I found myself navigating a world that didn't always offer kindness, struggling with my own sense of identity, and facing hardship with only hope to guide me.

"There's no harm in being afraid. You just have to not let it stop you." David's voice in my mind offered courage, a reminder that fear didn't have to control my destiny. Much like Davids journey, I knew the path ahead wouldn't be easy. But the strength to keep moving forward, despite the odds, was a lesson I could draw from his resilience. Just as David did, I learned to face the difficulties of my world, not as obstacles, but as a challenge to survive, to fight back in my own quiet way.

But even when the adventure in the books seemed far away, it kept me going, day by day. Through the pages of Treasure Island and Kidnapped, I could live other lives. I could sail the seas, face off with pirates, fight for my survival, and, like David, claim a kind of victory against the world. The strength of these characters gave me the courage to keep going when life felt difficult, when hunger gnawed at my stomach and the cold wrapped around me like a heavy blanket. They taught me that, no matter how impossible the odds seemed, there was always something worth fighting for.

My grandmother Emily whom I adored wrote a poem that I hold dear to this day. It was called Call of the Sea, and I remember how the words would echo in my mind as I read Stevenson tale of pirates and treasure hunts. I found a copy of the poem years later, and I wanted to share it with you, for it is tied to those quiet, peaceful moments when my mind would drift away from the hardship that surrounded us and into the vast, open sea.

Call of the Sea

by Emily Brownlee

The waves whisper his name at dawn,
While she clutches empty sheets, withdrawn.
Salt-kissed winds tug at his heart, as
ancient tides tear them apart.
Her tears fall like ocean spray,
As horizons steal him far away. Months
stretch long like endless shores, while
duty keeps him at his oars.
She curses Neptune's siren song,
That pulls him where he feels he belongs.
Their love caught in an endless dance, Between
duty and romance.
At night she walks the widow's walk,
Where seagulls cry and memories talk.
The lighthouse beam sweeps empty seas,
While loneliness rides each salted breeze.

His letters come on foreign winds,

Tales of ports and might-have-beens.
But paper words can't warm her bed

or ease the storm inside her head. The

sea, she knows, was his first love,

Before their vows to God above.

This mistress dressed in foam and blue,

Will always claim what she thinks is due.

So here she waits, as wives must do, while

oceans paint the world anew.

Her heart set sail that first goodbye,

Where sea meets endless, azure sky.

The words of Emily poem, so full of yearning and the ache of separation, connected with the world I found in Treasure Island and Kidnapped. Her words about the sea, the constant pull of duty, and the deep ache of separation felt like a mirror to the world I was living in. In some ways, my grandmother's poem was a balm for my own soul, echoing the longing for something better, for freedom from the struggles we faced every day. It spoke to the part of me that longed for adventure, for escape from the limits of my world, and for the kind of release that only stories and the imagination could offer.

Reading Treasure Island and Kidnapped was more than just a pastime it was a lifeline. In those books, I found not just a world of adventure, but a world where things could be. right, where good could conquer evil, and where treasure was not just gold but something worth pursuing something that made life feel full, even when the reality was so far removed from that promise.

In those nights, alone in my room with only the faint glow of the streetlight to guide me, I sailed the seas in my mind, leaving behind the hunger, the cold, and the hardship. And for a moment, I could forget it all and become part of a world where anything was possible.

Chapter 13

Into Care

It started as an ordinary morning. The kind where the canary-yellow sunlight felt like a lie, as if the world outside our window had missed the memo about the storm brewing inside our house. My siblings and I were playing in the garden, our laughter thin and fragile, like it might shatter if you listened too closely. My mum was inside, her silhouette sharp and still against the kitchen window, a statue frozen mid-thought. I didn't know it then, but she was waiting. The knock came, sharp and unkind, like a slap. Three quick raps against the front door, and everything changed. The door opened, and in walked a police officer, a police officer, and a gentleman social worker. Their presence was like a cold draft through the room. The uniforms of the police officers made the moment feel heavy, official, like this wasn't just a visit but a verdict. The social worker wore a soft-coloured jumper, his expression a mix of duty and discomfort. Their voices were too kind, their smiles too tight, as if rehearsed. I remember thinking they looked like the kind of people who handed out leaflets at the community centralized on the surface, but with something unsettling beneath.

At first, I didn't understand. My mum's lips moved, her words spilling out in a whisper that only they seemed to hear. She nodded a lot, her head bobbing like one of those dashboard dogs, and I could see the way her hands trembled as she reached for her cup of tea. The world outside the window seemed to hold its breath, the garden too green, the sky too blue.

Then I heard it. One word, slipping through the room like a knife 'jail.' I didn't know why my dad had been taken, only that he was gone, and suddenly everything that had felt solid turned to sand beneath my feet. The world tilted, and I found myself staring at the threadbare carpet, focusing on a patch where the pattern had worn away, as if I could disappear into that small, safe space. Here was no carpet just a stone floor, hard and cold underfoot. The only attempt at comfort was a musty old rug, a hand-me-down from one set of grandparents or the other. It had once been a pattern of reds and greens, but by then, it was mostly a muddle of stains and threadbare patches. The kind of rug that seemed to hold onto the smells of every room it had ever been in a bit of coal dust, a hint of damp, and a whiff of something stale, like old tobacco.

It lay crooked in the middle of the room, its edges curled up as if even it wanted to get away. If you weren't careful, you'd trip over it. I did, once, and caught a sharp cuff around the ear for my trouble. "Watch where you're going," my dad had snapped, as if the room were an obstacle course designed just for me to fail.

That old rug was the closest we had to a dining room table. My plate sat on it most nights, balanced on the uneven weave, and Id hunch over it, guarding my food from the dog. Not that the dog ever tried to take it he had more sense than I did. He would curl up on the edge of the rug, keeping his distance but close enough to share our little island of comfort.

When I sat there, knees pulled up, back to the wall, Id trace the patterns in the rug with my fingers. Id follow the worn threads like a maze, imagining I could find a way out if I just kept going. It was a silly game, but it helped. It was better than looking up, better than seeing the room as it really was bare, cold, and full of shadows.

They told us we were going on a trip. The kind of trip where you don't need to pack because they'll provide everything. The kind of trip you don't come back from. My little brother started to cry, and I wanted to tell him it was okay, but the words turned to dust in my mouth. My mum didn't say goodbye. She just stood there, her arms crossed, fingers digging into her sides as if she were holding herself together by sheer force of will.

The car smelled like vinyl and old coffee. I pressed my forehead against the cool glass of the window, watching the world outside blur and twist. The streets I knew so well where I had ridden my bike, where I had scraped my knees slid past, becoming nothing more than scenery. I tried to swallow the lump in my throat, but it sat there, heavy, and sharp.

The drive felt endless. I kept waiting for someone to say it was a mistake, for my mum to come running after us, her arms open wide. But the only voices were the murmured conversation of the adults in the front seat, their words muffled by the engine's hum. I stared at the door handle all the way there. It was an old, clunky thing the kind you had to pull up on with just the right amount of force. Not too hard, or it would stick, not too soft, or nothing would happen at all. Funny how something so ordinary could hold the promise of an escape.

I imagined reaching out, wrapping my fingers around it, and giving it a sharp tug. The door would swing open, and Id tumble out, rolling into the grass at the side of the road. Id imagined it so many times that I could almost feel the cool metal in my hand, the rush of air, the sudden, dizzying freedom of it.

But my hand never moved. It sat in my lap, balled into a fist so tight my nails dug into my palms. The pain was sharp and real a small defiance in a world where everything else felt out of my control. I was too scared to move, too numb to cry.

I wondered if they would even stop. Would the car screech to a halt, tires skidding, or would they keep driving, the empty space beside them just another problem solved? Would they tell people Id run away, or would they spin a different story, one where Id simply vanished, a cautionary tale whispered over tea and biscuits?

In the end, the door handle remained untouched. My escape was only ever in my head. And the car just kept going, taking me further away from everything I'd ever known.

No one explained anything. It was like being plucked out of a story halfway through, only to find out everyone else got to keep reading. I thought I'd been taken from all my family that they were still together, living their lives, while

I was the only one who had been plucked away, like a jigsaw piece that didn't fit any more.

Chapter 14

I Couldn't Even Take My Books

It wasn't just that I was gone. It was that they might not even notice. The world kept spinning, days rolled into nights, and I was the only one who had fallen off the edge. I wasn't just lost I'd been left behind, like a bookmark forgotten in a book that had already been returned to the library. The truth, of course, was less clean-cut. Over the years, I learned that my family had their own tangled knots of pain and confusion, their own versions of the story where they were the ones left behind. But back then, all I had was the sharp edge of loneliness, a blade that never dulled, and the nagging feeling that I was the only one who hadn't been given a script. Looking back, that was the day I learned that nothing is permanent. That the world can change with a single knock on the door. I built walls that day the kind you can't see but feel, a barrier between me and the rest of the world. I became an expert at keeping people at arm's length, always waiting for the ground to give way beneath me again. I didn't trust in 'forever' anymore because nothing ever was. Then I heard it. One word, slipping through the room like a knife 'jail.' I didn't know why my dad had been taken, only that he was gone, and suddenly everything that had felt solid turned to sand beneath my feet.

I had only heard of jail in the westerns I used to watch of the black and white TV. The world tilted, and I found myself staring at the threadbare carpet, focusing on a patch where the pattern had worn away, as if I could disappear into that small, safe space. They told us we were going on a trip. The kind of trip where you don't need to pack because they'll provide everything. The kind of trip you don't come back from. My little brother started to cry, and I wanted to tell him it was okay, but the words turned to dust in my mouth. My mum didn't say goodbye. She just stood there, her arms crossed, fingers digging into her sides as if she were holding herself together by sheer force of will. They drove us to the social work department, and as the car pulled away, I couldn't help but feel a wave of confusion and fear. It's a strange thing being taken from your parents the feeling of loss is something that I hope I'll never feel again. You always blame yourself I did not know what I had did wrong. I was separated from the family no one told me what was happening to my other siblings. I later found out we were all split up in the same way.

The engine hummed steadily as we drove toward Blackwood, twenty miles from our home. I had never heard of it I just knew that it seemed like an age. The landscape blurred past, each turn and bend in the road seeming to stretch on forever. I couldn't help but glance back, half-expecting to see our old home still in the distance, some trace of what had been left behind. But the car was taking us further away, and soon enough, all I could see were fields and trees. My heart felt tight in my chest, and I couldn't shake the feeling that something important, something precious, was slipping away.

When I arrived, I was greeted by a new foster family strangers who were supposed to take care of us now. The house was different from anything I had known. The Wimpy house was new, freshly painted with clean, white walls, and warm, welcoming rooms that smelled of wood polish and fresh linens. It was so different from the cold, dark rooms I was used to. Everything felt unfamiliar, strange, but there was something about it that made me hesitate. There was comfort in this new place, but it was also filled with a sense of uncertainty.

The hardest part, though, was that I was alone. Separated from all my siblings, I was in a new place, with unknown faces, and no one to lean on. I had always shared my life with them; felt their presence in everything I did. Now, that part of me was gone. The silence in my room felt louder than the noise of the outside world. I longed for the familiar laughter and arguments of my siblings; the shared moments of comfort we had always given each other. But now, I was by myself.

"This is your room now," the foster mother said warmly, her voice soft and inviting. She smiled at me, like she was trying to ease my worry. "Would you like to see it?" I felt as if I was betraying my family. I felt as if I had been stolen.

"Is... is it all mine?" I asked, barely able to believe what she was saying. My heart raced as I processed the idea of having my own room. A room I didn't have to share, a room with my name on it.

"All yours, lad. And theirs clean clothes in the drawer for you," she said, her words soothing the chaos inside me. I walked carefully into the room, afraid to touch anything, as if I might break something by just being there. It was so different from the place from which I had come. The walls were decorated with bright, welcoming colours, and the bed was made up neatly, with crisp sheets that smelled like fresh laundry. I felt like I didn't belong in this perfect, clean space. My hands hovered over the bedspread, too clean and too new. I was an impostor in my own life.

A sense of guilt twisted in my gut. I could hear my mum's voice in the back of my mind, sharp and accusing. "Living it up now, are you? Forgot where you came from already?" I felt as if enjoying this new room was a betrayal to my family. Who were they to steal me? I didn't trust them. I didn't need them. I hated them. I blamed them.

I felt like a thief in this room, like I'd stolen it from some other boy who truly deserved it. I wondered if I could ever feel at home anywhere, or if I'd always be searching for the door, ready to run.

Chapter 15

Distrust Misplaced

Another foster boy lived there too. He smiled at me, and though I was shy and unsure, we soon became friends. I whispered to him when we were alone how do we get out of here he looked at me confused. I spent the next couple of weeks watching them for the facades to slip. There was no shouting, hitting, threats, there must be something it felt strange to be just cared for. I had never felt so clean. I had never had a shower before, still don't like them, bloody things there is always a part of you that bloody cold. There was something comforting about having someone else in the house who was going through this same strange transition. We spent the afternoons exploring the house and its new rules, quietly getting to know each other, our shared experience providing a silent understanding between us. He was OK and he eased my feelings of dread.

The house smelled different clean, with the scent of cooking meals and furniture polish filling the air. It was so unfamiliar, yet it was a relief. There was a sense of order here, a sense of structure that was missing in my previous life. The family was kind to me, not overwhelming, but always there when I needed them. They gave me space, but they never left me alone in the dark. They were there when I needed to talk when I needed comfort.

The best part, though, was the food. I had never experienced anything like this before. Actual meals, not just creative uses for stale bread, volume three. They got me new clothes, clothes that fit, and they fed me foods I had never seen. I remember the first time I had an orange. The taste was unlike anything I had ever known, so sweet and refreshing that I couldn't believe it was real. I took a bite, and the juice exploded in my mouth, filling me with an unexpected joy. And the grapefruit I had never tasted anything so tangy and fresh. Each bite was like a new discovery, a small treasure in a world I was still learning to understand.

The family wasn't perfect, and things were far from easy, but in that house, for the first time in a long while, I felt a sense of comfort, even if it was only fleeting. I didn't know what the future held, or how long I would be there, but in that moment, I was given a small space to breathe. A space where I could begin to rebuild.

Chapter 16

Gratitude and Reflection

(I had to add this here it did not feel right thank them with everyone else at the end)

I have cherished these memories all my life. They were the brief moments of kindness that gave me the strength to keep going. But There's one thing I always wished I could have done: say thank you. I tried to get in touch; to reach out to let them know how much they meant to me, but I didn't know their names properly. When I was young, life was all about survival, and I couldn't think beyond the immediate need for safety and food. I didn't have the words then, but I have them now.

The family gave me a sense of security I had never known. They gave me warmth, clean clothes, and food that wasn't a reminder of how little I had. They gave me a room of my own, a place to rest and think, and they treated me like I mattered. In a world that felt uncertain, they were the constants that provided stability.

Years later, I got my care notes, and in them, I found a small insight that stayed with me forever. It was like the care workers had seen through everything I had been feeling. "Ian always needs space or he gets overwhelmed," it said. The simplicity of those two lines, so brief, yet so profound, meant more to me than anything else in those reports. It was a recognition of who I was, even before I understood it myself. They must have thought I was strange, needing to be alone, but they understood. And for that, I am forever grateful.

I may not have been able to say thank you then, but sincerely, I thank them now. They were beautiful, wonderful people who gave me something that I didn't know how to ask for: peace.

Chapter 17

Changes

School changed everything when I moved to Blackwood. For the first time, I looked like everyone else proper haircut, clean uniform, shoes without holes. No more cardboard stuffed in my shoes to keep the rain out, no more trying to hide the wear and tear of my old clothes. In some strange way, I felt like I had been given a chance to start over, a chance to fit in, to not be reminded constantly of the life I had left behind.

The playground was full of shouts, games, and laughter everything was different, but somehow, it all felt right. The other kids played together without a second thought, their voices blending into the background noise that became my new normal. Though I missed my grandparents and the comfort of my books, the change in my appearance made me feel like I was a part of something bigger, something I hadn't known was possible. I didn't stand out anymore. I wasn't the strange, shy kid in ragged clothes; I was just another kid at school, and for the first time, which felt like a gift.

That summer blazed bright and warm, the sun casting golden rays over everything. The wheat field behind the house grew tall, perfect for running, playing, and getting lost in the long grasses. It was a summer that seemed endless, full of promise. And in that time, my foster dad became a pivotal part of my life. He taught me three things that changed my world: guitar, chess, and rugby. The guitar was something I had never imagined picking up, but my foster dad showed me how to play, and though I had forgotten how by the time I left, the sound of the strings and the rhythm of the strums stayed with me. Chess became a game that kept my mind sharp, the satisfying click of the pieces on the board providing an escape, a sense of purpose. But rugby, rugby was different. It was something that I hadn't experienced with my own dad. We practiced in the field behind the house, the grass cools under our feet as we ran through drills. I'd try to tackle him, running as fast as I could, throwing myself into what I thought were hard tackles. He would laugh gently not at me, but with me, encouraging me even when I missed the mark. There was something freeing about it. I had never experienced that kind of play with my father. I had tried once, running at him with everything I had, hoping to prove myself, but instead, I hit him too hard. I remember the punch he threw at me in return, the blood on the floor, the feeling of being too much. My father's anger hit me hard, and my nose burst with the impact, blood streaming everywhere. I remember the terror in my chest, convinced in that moment that my dad would kill me. The blood seemed endless, and I could hear my siblings in the background, the chaos of it all blending into a blur of fear. This was nothing like the fun I had with my foster dad. With him, the laughter was light, genuine, and never came with the cost of violence. When I tackled him in rugby, it was part of the game, part of the fun. He liked to see me smile. I didn't have to worry about doing something wrong, I didn't have to fear his anger. I just played, and in those moments, I felt a freedom I'd never known.

Years later, when my son hit his grandfather too hard in a playful moment, the cycle came full circle. My father, unchanged, reacted with the same ferocity he had shown me. He hit my son back with the same violence, and I knew then that the past had not been left behind. That was the end of it. I made sure my children were never around him again.

I told them, "If you want to be in touch with him, you can. I'll never stop you." But thankfully, for the most part, they kept away. I had made my choice. I had seen the damage that kind of anger could do, and I wasn't going to let it touch my children. Id protect them from the cycle of violence that had marked my childhood. They deserved more than that.

Looking back, I am glad that the cycle ended with me.

Chapter 18

Brief Paradise

The community gala stands out in my memory like a photograph bleached by the sun, its edges fading but the core still vivid in my mind. It was a day of colour and sound, of costumes and laughter. Everyone was dressed up, and I was given the chance to be Jack Hawkins, my childhood hero. They handed me a proper fencing sword, the kind with a safety tip, and for the first time, I felt like I was part of something. I wasn't just the strange, quiet kid; I was Jack Hawkins, ready to fight pirates, to sail the high seas. I could feel the weight of the sword in my hand, the thrill of pretending I was on a grand adventure. The sun was hot, its rays beating down on the field where the gala was held, making the grass dry and golden underfoot. The air was filled with music and the laughter of children, a sound so full of life it erased the heaviness I had carried for so long.

For the first time in my life, I felt like I belonged somewhere. It wasn't just a fleeting feeling it was the first time I could truly relax, to be just a kid. The costumes, the games, the fun it all felt so natural. I was part of the crowd, playing alongside the other kids, no judgement, no differences, just laughter. I remember running through the grass, the sound of my friend's voices carrying across the field, and for those few hours, the world seemed perfect. I felt seen, valued, and like I mattered.

But, of course, it couldn't last.

One ordinary morning, everything changed. The social workers came to collect me again. They drove me to the social work office, the weight of the silence in the car so thick it felt suffocating. My parents were already waiting for me. There were no tearful goodbyes, no explanations, no discussion about what had happened, or why. The happiness I had felt just hours before at the gala was gone, replaced by a strange numbness that settled in my chest. Just like that, it was over. My brief paradise had vanished. The car ride home was silent except for the soft hum of the radio in the background, playing a song, I didn't remember. The passing scenery blurred by, and I couldn't bring myself to look at my parents. I didn't know what to say, didn't know what I was feeling. The sense of being torn from something that had felt like real belonging was too overwhelming. The house, the comfort, the safety everything I had come to know in my foster home felt like a dream fading away. I missed it already, even before I knew what it meant to lose it.

There was no warmth waiting for me when we got back to the house. The familiar walls felt colder, more distant. The room where I had once found safety and familiarity felt strangely alien. There was no welcoming smile from my foster mother, no gentle encouragement from my foster father. No soft laughter, no care. It was just silence. And that silence spoke louder than anything else. The separation from my foster parents was more than just physical it felt like the world had been pulled out from under me, and I was left with nothing but a vague sense of loss and confusion.

I wished more than anything that I could have stayed there, with them. They had given me more love and stability than I had ever known. They had taught me so much how to play guitar, how to think strategically with chess, how to laugh and enjoy life with rugby. They never judged me. They made me feel seen and loved something I never thought I would experience again. I missed them deeply, and though I didn't know how to express it then, I felt a deep yearning to return to their care, to that warmth, that peace. Years later, I would often think about those days, the warmth of that home, the laughter, the safety. I would wonder what might have happened if things had turned out differently. Could I have stayed? Would they have kept me? I never got to say goodbye, never got to thank them for showing me that love was possible, that I could belong. I wish I had been able to tell them how much they meant to me, how deeply I appreciated everything they had done for me. But all I had were the memories, memories that I would cherish for the rest of my life.

Chapter 19

The Broken Bank

Content Warning: *References to emotional abuse*

In my room, I opened my suitcase slowly, feeling the weight of what was inside. I took out Ralph gifts a small chess set and a rugby ball that doubled as a money bank. The ball was made of hard plastic, and as I held it, I felt the wear from use, the scuff marks that spoke of countless memories made in Blackwood. Inside, there were the pennies Ralph, and the family had helped me save. Not much money, but each coin felt like a small piece of the world I had briefly lived in a world where I was cared for, where I wasn't just another child lost in the cracks.

It wasn't just the pennies. It was everything Blackwood had been the warmth, the stability, the love. The ball and the chess set weren't just gifts; they were symbols of the safety I had found, the kindness and attention I had never known. It was a connection to a place where I had mattered, where I wasn't judged or forgotten.

But then, it all came crashing down.

One day, my father walked into the room. He looked down at the rugby ball, and something about the way he stood there his face twisting with anger made my stomach drop. "What's this then?" he demanded, his voice sharp and biting.

"It's mine," I whispered, barely able to speak. "They gave it to me."

Before I could say another word, he grabbed the ball from my hands. I felt a shock run through me, a panic building in my chest. "Ungrateful little cunt," he hissed. "Think your better than us now?"

The words hit me like a physical blow, cold and sharp. I didn't know how to defend myself, didn't know how to explain that it wasn't about being better it was about being loved, about feeling safe for the first time. But I couldn't say any of that. I was frozen in place, unable to speak, my mind racing with a thousand thoughts, none of them coming out.

And then, without warning, he tore open the rugby ball. The hard plastic split under his hands, and I heard the sharp crack as it broke open. The pennies spilled out, scattering across the floor, rolling in every direction. The sound of them hitting the ground felt like my heart shattering. Each coin, each penny that had come to represent the care and love of Blackwood, now felt like a symbol of everything being taken from me.

"Ungrateful," he spat, his words bitter and cutting. "Think your better than us?" His voice was like a knife, each syllable carving deeper into my chest. I watched as he turned and walked out of the room, leaving the broken pieces of the rugby ball scattered on the floor. The plastic fragments, sharp and jagged, lay in stark contrast to the warmth they once held.

I stood there in silence, my chest aching, the world spinning. It wasn't just the ball that was broken, it was me. My heart, my connection to Blackwood, was shattered in that instant. My father had taken the one thing I had left that was good, that was mine. The warmth, the safety, the love I had briefly felt it was all gone in a moment, swept away by his cruelty.

Years later, and even now, I still feel the weight of that loss like an emotional hangover you just can't shake, no matter how much life experience you chug.

The system that had taken me from Blackwood, which had placed me back with my parents, betrayed me. They didn't ask me what I wanted, didn't ask for my opinion. They didn't see me. I was just a child, but my needs, my desires, my rights were ignored. As I write this, tears are falling.

Even after all this time, the pain is still there. I was torn away from the one place I felt safe, and the people who should have cared for me who should have protected me did the opposite. They broke my heart. I had nothing left from Blackwood. Nothing to hold onto but the broken pieces of a plastic rugby ball and the empty feeling of betrayal. And that emptiness hasn't fully gone away. Even now, it lingers, a quiet ache that I carry with me.

Chapter 20

Back to Nothing

Content Warning: *References to emotional abuse and physical trauma*

The return home, everything was different, I didn't have my ravine to play in. Another house this one had nothing. It was beside a busy road so I was limited of the playing I could do. The return home brought new responsibilities, ones for which I wasn't prepared. My mother became pregnant again, and as the months passed, I found myself kept from school. I wasn't allowed to go, not for the lessons, not for the break, not for anything. I became the family's runner to the shops, to the butcher, wherever they needed something. For nine months, I was the one who ran errands, the one who had to take care of everything.
I wasn't a child anymore; I was expected to be an adult. I should have been at school, should have been playing with other kids, but instead, I was the one carrying bags, picking up groceries, running to my uncles shop for mince or stew meat for free. My uncle, the butcher, gave us what we

needed without charge another reminder of how little we had, and how much I had to grow up too fast. I was 8 and walking the mile and a half into town. I knew every step I used to pretend I was a secret agent, and I had to hide from all the cars. My parents had told me to get there and straight back.

The truancy officer's visits became regular. His concerned face at our door was a reminder that I wasn't where I should have been. His presence was like a shadow, a constant ticking clock, marking the time when I should have been in school, learning, growing like every other child. But instead, I was learning how to run errands, how to be invisible, how to survive.

One day, feeling proud of my independence, I walked the mile and a half into town to get the meat from my uncle's shop. The walk felt like something important, something that gave me purpose, which made me feel like I could manage it all. I could almost feel the pride swelling in my chest as I carried the bag back, feeling like I was part of the adult world. But when I got back late to collect my sister from school, my mother's hand quickly reminded me of my place. The slap across my face was swift and stinging, a punishment for being late, for doing something wrong without even knowing it. That night, I lay in bed, my face still stinging, and I prayed for Ralph to come and get me. I longed for the comfort of Blackwood, for a place where I felt valued. But some prayers go unanswered. Mine did. At this time, though, there was no school to see my condition, no one to notice. The scabies had come back, worse than ever. I felt it crawling under my skin, itching so bad it seemed like I couldn't stop scratching. I remember the sensation of my hair crawling, too. Every inch of my scalp itched, and no matter how hard I scrubbed, it never felt clean. I can still feel it now when I think of it the way my head crawled with that feeling, as if the bugs were living in me, inside my very bones. The worst part was that no one cared enough to help. There were no doctors, no teachers, no one to protect me. I was just left to suffer in silence, just another part of the mess that my life had become Then one day, the big van came. The men arrived, taking everything, we had and putting it out onto the street. We didn't have much, but what we did have was ours. It wasn't much, but it was everything. We stood there, wandering aimlessly, as my mother and father blamed each other for the mess they had created. They fought in front of us, arguing about everything and nothing, as if the destruction of our lives was anyone's fault but their own.

Finally, my father had had enough. His anger flared, and when he couldn't blame her anymore, he turned to violence. He punched her once more, the impact sending her to the floor. Then, as if she were nothing but a thing to be discarded, he kicked her full on in the face. The sound of it was sickening, like something inside me breaking. I should have felt sorry for her. I should have felt something, anything. But I didn't. I couldn't. Every time she came near me, every time I saw her face, I felt physically sick. The anger, the hatred I felt for her was overwhelming, and yet, I couldn't stop it. She had never been a mother to me. She had been a source of pain, of fear, of anger.

And even after all of this, even after everything that had happened, the worst part remained: my mother. Up until her death, I always felt the same when she was near me. I couldn't stand her presence. This is the only way I can describe it, it wasn't a feeling of hatred it was fear and nausea. I was physically sick when she came into the same room as me, though it wasn't often. Every time she came close, I could feel the bile rise in my throat, my stomach turning, my body wanting to shut down. I couldn't love her, couldn't feel sympathy for her, and every inch of me recoiled from her. The abuse, the neglect, the hurt everything she had put me through left me with nothing but this overwhelming disgust and sickness when she was near. That night, I didn't cry for her. I didn't cry for anyone. I had cried enough over the years, cried enough for a lifetime. All I could do was stand there, numb, watching as the world around me fell apart. The violence, the chaos it all felt too familiar, too much a part of me. And I knew, without a doubt, that I would never feel safe again. This pattern of violence continued throughout my life. It lasted through my childhood, and even into adulthood, this visceral reaction to her presence never left me. Every time I saw her, every time she came near me, that sick feeling returned. It wasn't something I could control. It was something that had been built over years of hurt, years of abuse.

I couldn't shake it, couldn't stop it. It was a part of me, a part I couldn't escape. My father didn't bring the same feeling of being sick. But he gave me a huge lesson one I will cherish. I never ever wanted to grow up like my dad. I can remember them taking us to the social work department and threatening to leave all us kids there. The social work can fucking feed you he said. That never happened that night we stayed at my grandfathers the gardener I went to school the next day with my sister.

Chapter 21

The White Building

Content Warning: *References to institutional care and abuse*

The Tannoy crackled through the school halls, its sharp static cutting through the air as my name was called. "Ian Hughes, can you come to the office, please?" I had heard my sisters name called earlier, but at that moment, I didn't understand what it meant. There was no warning, no explanation. I just followed the instructions, the sense of unease building in my chest like a knot tightening with every step. When I walked into the headmaster's office, the sight of two police officers and a social worker sitting there made my stomach turn. Their faces were stern, their eyes cold. I didn't know what was going on, and my sister wasn't there. I had no idea why. I just stood there, frozen, waiting for someone to tell me what was happening. But no one spoke. Their silence filled the room, a heavy, suffocating weight. They took me away, and before I could understand what was happening, I found myself in a car, being driven to a big white building in my birth town a place I had only.

heard whispered about but never actually seen. The building was huge, looming over me, with an air of coldness that made my skin crawl. It felt impersonal, like a place meant to erase who you were. Its windows were dark and unblinking, giving nothing away. I had never imagined that this was where I would end up, and now that I was here, I didn't know what to think.

The building itself was new, built in the sixties or early seventies. It was clean and tidy, the kind of place that still smelled faintly of fresh paint and industrial cleaning products. The walls were smooth and white, the floors a polished linoleum that squeaked underfoot. Compared to what I was used to, it should have felt like a step up. It was basic but well-kept, with neat rows of chairs and orderly corridors. On the surface, it was lovely.

But a home isn't just what it looks like it's how it feels. And this place felt worn. There was a sense of tiredness in the air, a weight that pressed down on everything. It was as if everyone here had given up, like the building itself had resigned to being a stop gap, a holding place for lost things. It was clean, yes, but empty. There was no warmth, no life.

It was a shell of a home, lacking the soul that made a place feel safe.

Inside, the walls were stark white, the floors hard and cold underfoot. The building smelled of disinfectant, a sharp, clinical smell that filled my nose and made me want to gag. There was no comfort, no warmth. I felt like I had been dropped into a world that wasn't mine, a world where I didn't belong. Everything around me felt like it was designed to make you disappear, to make you feel small, like you were nothing more than a number.

When we arrived in our assigned room, my younger brother was already there. He was sitting on one of the two beds, looking lost. His face was pale, his eyes wide with confusion. His feet dangled off the edge of the bed, too small for the world he had been thrust into.

Ian where are we? he asked, his voice trembling with fear.

I didn't have an answer. I was just as confused as he was. I didn't know why we were here, or what I had done wrong. My stomach churned with fear, the weight of the unknown pressing down on me. I was just a kid, I didn't understand any of this. All I could feel was the deep sense of confusion, that overwhelming fear of not knowing why I was being taken away.

Were on an adventure, I lied, trying to make it sound like everything was fine, trying to protect him from the fear I could feel eating at me. I didn't want him to see how scared I was. I told him stories of peter pan and the lost boys. Were just here with all the lost boys I was ten and told my brother that. I'm scared, he whispered, his voice breaking. Don't be, I said, forcing a smile even though I didn't feel brave at all. I'm here with you. I'll always protect you. The words were hollow, but I had to say them. I couldn't let him see how terrified I was.

But the truth was, I was shitting myself. I didn't know what I had done wrong, why I was here, or what would happen next. I had no control over any of it. All I knew was that I wasn't in school anymore, and now I was in a place that felt so alien, so wrong.

That night I got scrubbed in-between my fingers and my hair had a chemical put in it. And what is called a bone comb ran through my hair harshly it was so sore. I thought he was ploughing my head. There was absolutely no feeling that I was a kid on the other end of that comb.

The days in the white building blurred together. The routine was strict and unyielding. Wake up, line up, eat, sit quietly, go to bed. The food was tasteless, Grey, and lukewarm, served on plastic trays that rattled as they were slid across tables. The adults never smiled. Their voices were sharp, quick to cut down anyone who strayed from the rules. I learned quickly to keep my head down, to make myself as small as possible. The other lads there were good lads. But there was a hierarchy and if you stepped out of line you either quickly stepped back in or fought. Not for the first time I chose when to pick my battles. The nights were the worst. In the silence, fear took on a shape, wrapping around me in the dark. I would listen to my brothers breathing, shallow and uneven, and whisper stories to him, tales of knights and dragons, of heroes who always won. I told him that we were just passing through, that soon we would be home, but I didn't believe it myself. I told him to imagine we were on a secret mission, that we were spies and this was just part of the plan. It was a lie, but it was the only comfort I had to offer.

This building, the white place, was the beginning of something I couldn't yet comprehend. But it was also the place where my brothers fear, and trauma worsened. He confided in me later, sharing that he had never felt safe in his life. He still wakes up at night, his hand instinctively reaching to stick his fist down his throat, trying to gag on something that isn't there anymore. He remembers being force-fed, something that happened often, a punishment, a way of breaking his spirit. The images are burned into his memory, and they haunt him still. I tried to protect him as best I could, but we were small, and they were all so big. The world felt out of control, and no one ever listened. No one saw what was happening. I couldn't stop it, no matter how hard I tried. The feeling of helplessness, of not being able to protect him from the horrors we were both enduring, is something I carry with me still.

After all the threats throughout my life, it seemed inevitable that we would end up there the bad boy's home. The endless threats, the verbal abuse, the promises of punishment if we didn't fall in line, finally became a reality. It wasn't a place I had ever imagined myself going, but it felt like there was no way out, no escape from the cycle. It was like I had been marching toward that moment my entire life, and finally, there I was.

I didn't know what would come next, but I knew that the pain and the struggle hadn't ended. We were just in a new place now, one that felt as cold and isolating as everything else in my life. The feeling of being abandoned, of being discarded, was overwhelming. But this time, I had no choice but to face it. School was a relief I enjoyed school I like my teacher she was young relatable, and she had time for me. She gave me a part in the school play that year. The play was calamity Jane I remember laughing as I sang whip crack away, whip crack away.

Chapter 22

Rules Rules and More Rules

Content Warning: *Institutional Abuse, Forced Feeding, Withholding Food*

The white building held its secrets well. From the outside, it looked clean and orderly a modern institution, built in the sixties or early seventies, with its smooth white walls and well-kept gardens. But beneath the surface, behind the polished linoleum floors and the neat rows of chairs, there was a different story one of control, punishment, and silence.

One of the first routines I learned was bath time. It wasn't the kind of bath time I had known before, with warm water, privacy, and the gentle hum of household noises in the background. Here, it was a line-up a row of small, vulnerable bodies waiting their turn, naked and exposed. We stood, skin prickling with the chill of the tile floors, eyes fixed forward because looking around only made it worse. There was no place for modesty or dignity, only the shuffle forward, step by step, as each child took their turn in the bath. This was defiantly not how I had a bath and shower in Blackwood this was something else. They would even let us stand with our pants on. It was humiliating the bastard every now and again used to crack your ass with a rolled tea towel. It bloody stung I hated him he was a dick. I learned quickly not to resist. Those who cried or tried to cover themselves were met with sharp words or rough hands. The adults didn't see us as children just as tasks to be managed, problems to be solved. The water was never quite warm enough, the soap harsh against the skin. There was no softness, no care just a brisk efficiency that made me feel more like livestock being hosed down than a boy being cared for. Ice seen cattle getting hosed down with more care.

But it was the hair washing I dreaded most. They would hold me still, their hands gripping my head in a way that felt too familiar, too much like my mother had once done. The water splashed over my face, cold and unrelenting, and I would panic, my mind dragging me back to a time when being held under the water was not about washing but about control, about fear. My scalp would burn from the brutal scrubbing, my hair twisted and pulled, my neck straining as I tried to keep my face above the water. I could swim, I could go under water but only on my own terms, when I chose to. Bath time took that choice away, and with it, any sense of safety.

Food, too, was a weapon. Meals were served on plastic trays, Grey and tepid, the kind of food that sat heavily in your stomach. But not everyone got the same. If you had been 'bad,' if you had broken a rule or spoken out of turn, food was withheld. A skipped meal, a smaller portion hunger used as punishment. I learned to chew slowly, to make each bite last, because I never knew when the next plate might come.

Being force-fed was worse. It happened when the staff decided you were being difficult, when you refused to eat or showed even the slightest defiance. They would hold you still, a hand on the back of your head, spoonsful pushed into your mouth whether you wanted them or not. The food was thick and tasteless, and the sensation of it sliding down my throat made me gag. But spitting it out wasn't an option. You learned to swallow, to keep it down, because the consequences of not doing so were worse.

There was a garden attached to the building a small patch of green that seemed to belong to another world. It was a place where the two Dalmatians, owned by the matron in the adjoining flat, would play. I used to love watching them. They were full of life, their black and white coats a blur as they chased each other, tongues lolling, eyes bright.

They didn't know about punishment or hunger. They didn't know what it was like to be afraid all the time.

But after I ran away, the garden was closed to me. The door remained shut, the gate locked. I would press my face to the window, watching the dogs bound through the grass, free in a way I could only imagine. Being denied that small joy was another kind of punishment a reminder that I had crossed a line, that I was no longer allowed even the smallest of comforts.

The adults called it discipline. They said it was for our own good, that rules had to be followed, that structure was important. But it never felt like care. It felt like control, like they were taking pieces of us away, one rule, one punishment at a time. The white building was a place where you learned to stay small, to make yourself invisible. It was a place where the outside world couldn't see what happened, where the truth lay buried beneath layers of order and routine.

Looking back, I realise how wrong it was. How none of it should have happened. But at the time, I didn't know any different. I thought it was normal to feel hungry, to be afraid of bath time, to long for the simple joy of a dog's wagging tail. I thought it was normal to feel like a ghost, half-seen and half-heard, drifting through the halls of a building that felt more like a cage than a home. And yet, somehow, I survived. I found small rebellions, tiny sparks of resistance. I would save crumbs of bread, hide them under my pillow, a secret stash against the hunger. I would close my eyes and imagine the garden, the soft grass under my feet, the dogs nudging my hand for a pat. I built a world in my head where the white building didn't exist, where I was just a boy, safe and free.

Chapter 23

The Day Elvis Died

Content Warning: *This chapter contains descriptions of assault and abuse.*

I remember exactly where I was when Elvis died. It was in the big sitting room, the one with the colour television. The news crackled from the screen: "Elvis Presley, the King of Rock and Roll, has died at his Grace land mansion..." "Turn that up," one of the staff called from the doorway, lighting a cigarette. "Can't believe the King is dead." It was a strange moment, one that should have been filled with shock, with people mourning the loss of a cultural icon. Instead, it felt like nothing more than a brief distraction from the grim reality that I was living. The whispers began almost immediately as soon as the staff member stepped outside. The words were sharp, like knives, cutting through the air. The hostility was palpable, and I had learned long ago to keep my head down. But that didn't stop the older boy from stepping forward, his voice laced with venom. "Oi, you. Get up here."

"Leave me alone," I managed to say, my voice barely a whisper, but it wasn't enough." Get up on that table. Now. "He screeched. When I hesitated, his grip tightened on my throat. I felt the air leave my lungs, my heart racing with fear. "Please don't," I whispered, my voice shaking. "Shut it," he hissed, his fingers digging into my skin.

"Or your little brother's next."

I knew in that moment that my life was not my own. It had never really been mine, not in this place. The others watched, some laughing, some turning away, indifferent to the cruelty. "Look at him crying. "Look at the wee wank cry. "Nobody's going to help you here."he mocked I tried to block it all out, tried to imagine I was somewhere else, anywhere else. But it was impossible. His voice, cold and commanding, was all I could hear. He pulled down my pyjamas and forced me onto the table, his words a twisted mockery of power and control. "I'll make the wee wank wank," he said, his grip never loosening. The pain was unbearable, a feeling I can't even put into words. My body betrayed me, and the blood my bloodstained my hand. It was too much, more than I could comprehend, and I was lost in the shame, the fear, the confusion. The physical pain wasn't the worst of it. It was the emotional weight, the violation that I carried with me long after it ended. The frenulum was piperidine modern parlance the banjo string. I have never been so violated. Nothing could get worse than that. I was wrong. Later that night, my brother's small voice came from the other bed: "Ian? Are you okay? "I'm fine," I lied, my voice thick with emotion, with something I couldn't name. "Try to sleep." "I'm scared. "Don't be," I whispered, fighting the tears that threatened to break through. "I won't let anyone hurt you. I promise. "But I knew, deep down, that there was nothing I could do to stop the cycle. The darkness seemed endless, and the words "I promise" felt hollow, empty, in the face of everything that had happened. In the distance, I could hear Elvis's voice, still playing somewhere down the hall: "Love Me Tender." The irony wasn't lost on me, even then. Love was something I couldn't comprehend. Tenderness was something I had never known in this place, never felt in the hands that had used me.

The next morning, at breakfast, the questions started: "Why are you walking funny? "Just tired," I said, avoiding their eyes, refusing to let anyone see the truth that weighed so heavily on my body, they were just taking the piss.

Looking back, I realise how much innocence I had lost that

day. Everyone was crying that Elvis had died, mourning a man who had given the world music and joy, while I hid my wound, afraid to let anyone see. The world outside was grieving for a celebrity. But inside, I was grieving for something deeper a loss that could never be healed by a song.

And I couldn't help but think, this never happened to Jack Hawkins, the brave boy in Treasure Island, or David Balfour, the adventurous soul from Kidnapped. They were heroes, living lives of adventure and courage, sailing the seas, and overcoming obstacles. They had purpose, strength, and the kind of futures I could never imagine. They never had to endure the things I had been forced to face. They never had their innocence stripped away in the dark, filthy corners of some forgotten institution. The heroes in those books didn't have their bodies marked with shame; they didn't feel the sting of betrayal, the way I had been made to feel worthless, used, and small. They got to be heroes, while I was just trying to survive. Shame was a heavy blanket, draped over my shoulders, weighing me down. It wasn't just a feeling it was a part of me, threaded through my skin, woven into the fabric of my being. I carried it everywhere. It sat with me when I ate, followed me into my dreams, and whispered in my ear when I was alone. It told me I was dirty, that I was nothing.

It made sure I knew that whatever had happened to me was my own fault, that I had somehow invited it, deserved it. I thought back to my days in the ravine, back when I still had dreams. Real dreams, not the kind that come at night and leave you waking up cold and lost. I used to imagine a world where I was the brave one, the one who escaped, who found treasure, who was more than just a boy with scuffed knees and empty hands. I used to think that if I climbed high enough, if I swung out far enough over the river, I could escape. I could soar.

But those dreams were gone now. They had slipped away like the rivers current, leaving me stranded on the shore. I wasn't big. I wasn't clever. I was just a wee boy broken and empty. The kind of kid you would pass on the street and not look twice at. The kind of boy who didn't get to be a hero in any story, not even his own.

The shame wasn't just in my mind it was in my bones. It was in the way I moved, shoulders hunched, eyes down. It was in the way I spoke, voice quiet and careful, as if the wrong word might give me away. I had become an expert at hiding, not just from the world but from myself. Id learned to blend into the background, to be nothing more than a shadow. Because shadows couldn't be hurt. Shadows couldn't feel.

And the worst part? The shame was a thief. It stole my memories, twisted them into something ugly. It took the few good moments I had the smell of tomatoes in a warm greenhouse, the swing over the river, the sun on my face and turned them into ghosts. I couldn't trust them. I couldn't trust myself. Shame had a way of turning everything sour, of making me question whether those good things had ever been real, or if I had made them up just to survive.

Shame told me I wasn't allowed to dream. It told me I wasn't allowed to hope. It kept me small, trapped in a story where I was the villain, the one who had brought it all upon himself. And every time I tried to push back, to find a crack in the walls it had built around me, it whispered in my ear, reminding me that I would always be nothing more than the boy who wasn't good enough to be loved.

I often wondered what it was supposed to look lifelike. Was it supposed to feel like a hero's journey, like the books I had read, where challenges were overcome and the bad guys were defeated? Was I ever supposed to feel like I belonged in the world, like there was hope? Or was I always supposed to feel this emptiness, this unbearable heaviness that weighed on me, a burden of memories and pain?

Some wounds leave no visible scars, but they never truly heal. They're buried deep, hidden beneath layers of silence and pain. But they remain, lingering like ghosts, long after the tears have dried.

Chapter 24

The Flight

Content Warning: *References to trauma and guilt*

Dawn hadn't yet broken when I made my choice. The house was still, heavy with unspoken threats and the residue of yesterday's violence. It was always their violence, looming like a shadow over every corner of our lives. My brother's soft breathing from the next bed made my heart ache. He was so small, so innocent, and I knew what would happen if I stayed. I could feel the weight of it, the never-ending cycle that had already taken so much from us both. "I'm sorry," I whispered to his sleeping form, the words barely audible in the dark. "I can't take you with me." That decision would carve itself into my conscience, a scar that time would never fully heal. I left him behind, knowing that the same hands that hurt me would find him too. But I also knew that I couldn't carry him, not in this world, not on this road. There were too many dangers ahead, and I couldn't protect him the way I wanted to.

The morning air bit sharp and clean as I slipped out, carrying nothing but the clothes on my back and guilt in my heart. I didn't dare take anything else, knowing that everything else would weigh me down. I needed to be light, to move fast. Two days of freedom stretched ahead a lifetime to a child, a blink to the adult I've become. "Just keep walking," I told myself, the words more of a command than advice. Each step took me further from danger, but also further from my brother. The road seemed endless, marked only by the rhythm of my feet and the weight of my choices. My grandparents' building loomed ahead, familiar yet forbidden, a reminder of all I had lost. I approached the alleyway that led to the bin cupboard, the only place I could hide. The bin cupboard became my sanctuary a small, concrete cave that smelled of refuse and desperation. It wasn't much, but it was mine. I arranged newspapers I had stolen into a makeshift bed, trying to ignore the cold, trying to ignore the hunger that clawed at my stomach. The papers crinkled under me, their headlines a harsh reminder of a world still spinning outside my small refuge. The ink smudged my hands, a stain that seemed to sink into my skin, just like everything else I carried. "This is temporary," I whispered to myself, trying to convince myself that this would only be a short stay. The headlines on the newspapers spoke of Elvis's death, and even here, I couldn't escape the memory. Elvis was gone, and his voice still haunted the background of my existence, filling every empty moment, every moment of loneliness. Hunger became my constant companion, sharper than the cold that seeped through the paper blankets. I learned to track the routines of the street: 5:30 AM: The baker's van 6:00 AM: Milk deliveries 6:15 AM: My chance.

The first theft was the hardest. I couldn't bring myself to take much, but it was enough a bottle of milk, still cold with morning dew, and two rolls. It wasn't enough to fill the gnawing emptiness, but it was something. Every bite was a battle satisfaction mixed with guilt. Each roll burned my conscience more than it filled my stomach. The hunger, the stealing, it all seemed like one big blur of survival, until I could feel the taste of guilt at the back of my throat. Every day, I stood before my grandparents' door, hand raised to knock. The brass doorbell gleamed in the morning light a promise of warmth, of safety, a promise I wasn't sure I could accept. Pride and fear fought their daily battle: Pride whispered: "You can manage this alone." Fear countered: "They'll send you back."

The doorbell gleamed, a brass promise of warmth and safety. But each time my finger neared it, I thought of the trouble I would cause, the questions they would ask, and these were answers I couldn't give. I couldn't tell them the truth couldn't show them what I had become, what I was hiding. So, I stayed away.

Nights were the worst. In the darkness of the bin cupboard, my brother's face haunted me his wee face, his trusting eyes, how small he was. He was still so young, so vulnerable, and I had left him behind. "He's safer there," I repeated like a mantra, trying to believe it, trying to convince myself that I had made the right choice. "They won't hurt him like they hurt me."

But the guilt remained, a constant companion in my concrete refuge. I could see his face whenever I closed my eyes. Every passing car might carry searching police officers, my grandparents, anyone who might report me. I had no way of knowing if they were looking for me, but it didn't matter. The fear and guilt were all-consuming. I learned to become invisible, to move like a shadow between empty streets, empty alleyways, and my bin shelter. I became a part of the landscape something nobody saw, nobody cared about. It was survival, nothing more. I learned to sleep sitting up, how to keep warm with paper, how to avoid being seen. And I learned to despise Elvis, for reminding me of everything I couldn't have, everything I couldn't be. And love me tender your having a laugh. But a midst all of this, there was one place I could escape to, if only for a moment a greenhouse full of tomatoes I found on my way back to Hamilton. When everything became too much, when the weight of the world felt unbearable, I would slip away to that place. I never disturbed anything or stole anything; I didn't need to. I just needed the smell of the plants, the way the air was thick with green, the way the world seemed to stand still in there. It reminded me of my grandfather, the gardener, who had always been warm and kind to me. I would stand in that greenhouse, inhaling the earthy scent, letting the quietness calm my mind. His presence lingered in those plants, in the smell of the tomatoes ripening under the glass. I loved him. I still did. Sadly, he passed away when I was 14, and I never got to tell him what he meant to me. I never got the chance to thank him for the safety he gave me, the warmth that had been my anchor in the storm. Now, all I had left was the memory of that long gone greenhouse.

But the hardest lesson was about love the kind of love that can tear you apart, make you leave behind what matters most, all in the name of survival. Days later, I would learn my brother had been safe, just as I had hoped. But the weight of leaving him never lifted.

When I look back now, I see that I learned something I could never fully understand at the time. Sometimes, just sometimes, the bravest choice feels like cowardice, the right decision hurts the most, and love means not letting anyone know how much your brother means to you. I didn't want any of this to happen to him. I had to keep my distance. I had to let him stay where he was, safe, even if I couldn't be there to protect him.

This was my other grandfathers house he worked in the steel works. My grandmother worked in Rolls Royce. My auntie working in a factory with sewing machines. I couldn't go to my other grandparents they would have been kinder, but I thought my mum and dad would be there. I die than going there. The Weight of Silence The nights were the hardest. When the world went quiet, and I was left alone with my thoughts. Id curl up in the bin cupboard, pull my jacket tight around me, and listen to the sounds of the street distant cars, the rustle of leaves, the hum of a city that didn't know I existed. I thought of my grandfather, his voice in my head, telling me stories about the mines, about hard work and grit. 'You've got to dig deep, son,' he would say. And so, I did. I dug into myself, into the stubbornness that ran deep in my bones. I wasn't going back. Not ever. On the second day, the fear started to dull, turning into a strange kind of resolve. I began to map out the streets in my head, learning which shops left food out, which corners were safe to hide. I became part of the landscape, just another shadow slipping between the cracks. And with each step, I felt a little stronger, a little more like myself. Whoever that was. Whoever I might become.

I couldn't knock on the door. I was scared. My hand hovered in the air, fingers curled into a tight fist that refused to move. The door seemed to loom over me, its chipped paint and worn handle a barrier too high to cross. What if they opened it and saw through me, saw the mess I was? What if they slammed it in my face, or worse, took me back? My feet felt heavy, cemented to the ground, but my chest was hollow, a yawning pit of fear and shame. I turned away, the weight of the door pressing against my back as I slipped back into the shadows. Safer there. Always safer. The bin cupboard kept me dry I learned if you get newspaper and put it on the ground its comfier and if you stick some rolled up it can function as a pillow.

Chapter 25

Caught and Punished

Content Warning: *This chapter contains references to punishment and emotional abuse.*

When the neighbour finally found me, he stayed below my grandparents' house, his face blank at first. Recognition dawned slowly, as I explained who I was. "I am Jocks and Evelyns grandson, I'm Barbara nephew," I said quietly, the words coming out like an apology. His face softened, but I saw the confusion and concern in his eyes. I wasn't sure what he thought of me then what he thought of the boy standing there in rags, hungry, dirty, and broken. His kitchen was warm, a small, comforting place in a world that had been so cold to me. The smell of breakfast, the promise of food, felt like paradise like something I could never really have, but had found again, if only for a moment. I hadn't realised how desperately I needed that warmth, that kindness, until I stepped into it. I never even got to see my grandparents or auntie. I must have missed them when they came home. I would imagine one of my grandparents would have a phone call at work. Instead of can't wait to see my grandson. They phoned the police. In all the time I was in care I never got a visit neither did my younger brother. The police arrived soon after. They'd been searching for me for two days, their faces hard and accusatory. I felt the air in the room grow heavy, suffocating, as they stormed in, their boots making harsh sounds on the wooden floor.

They were blunt, cruel in their words. Wasting our time, one of them muttered, his eyes sharp and cold. We have been looking for you everywhere, and this is where we find you? Do you think you can just run away and disappear? Their words hit me like physical blows, but they didn't matter. In that moment, I didn't care. They didn't know anything.

They didn't understand what I had just survived. I had been free, even if for just two days, and nothing they could say or do would take that away.

But back at the home, punishment came swiftly. It was more than I had expected, and it was more than I could bear. One of the staff members held my hand over the sterilising sink, the metal biting into my skin. The heat of the sink was unbearable, a warning, a reminder of the power they held over me. The searing pain was just the beginning, the first taste of what would come if I ever ran again.

The cruel irony of it all didn't escape me. They punished me for daring to take control of my own life, for daring to feel free, even if just for a moment. But even during the pain, I couldn't forget those two days. The taste of stolen rolls, sweeter than any meal served in that white building. The warmth of the neighbour's kitchen, the kind smile he gave me, the hope that had flickered, even if just for an instant.

That hope, which fleeting taste of freedom, couldn't be erased by the heat of the sterilising sink or the cruel words of the police. It stayed with me. No matter how many times they punished me, no matter how many times they tried to break me, they couldn't take away the memory of that small, stolen piece of peace. And that, in the end, was what kept me going. They had their control, their punishment, but they didn't have my spirit. It was still there, buried deep, just waiting for the next chance to escape.

Chapter 26

The Christmas Miracle

Content Warning: *This chapter contains references to institutional life and abuse.*

Strangely, amid all the darkness, one of my brightest memories comes from that place. Christmas brought an unexpected joy my first real toys, gifts from local businesses, and a man dressed as Santa Claus. These weren't hand-me downs from other children; they were new. For the first time, I could hold something that was mine and mine alone.

A toy that hadn't been worn out by others, which didn't come with the ghosts of other children's hands on it. I could play with something without wondering if it was going to break or if someone else had already had their turn with it.

The presents came from local businesses that had donated them to the children's home, a small gesture of kindness in a world that rarely offered anything for free. A doll. A toy car. Simple things, but to me, they were treasures. There were no lies to tell when I went back to school after the holidays. For once, I didn't have to pretend about what I had gotten. I didn't have to say, oh, I got this from my uncle, or This was a hand-me-down from someone else. This time, I could speak the truth and say, I got this for Christmas.

For this one day, the harsh rules softened. For this one day, the institution seemed to step back, just a little, and we were allowed to be children, not inmates of an institution, not faceless numbers in a system that saw us as burdens. It was as if time itself had stopped, and for a few fleeting hours, we were given permission to feel joy, to laugh, to be innocent, to simply be children.

The Christmas tree stood in the corner of the common room, its branches weighed down with brightly coloured tinsel and mismatched baubles. The lights blinked in a rhythm that was somehow soothing, like a heartbeat that reminded me, however briefly, that life could have a pulse of hope. The smell of pine, mixed with the warmth of the fire, filled the room, creating a rare sense of comfort. For once, the air didn't taste like fear.

And then, there was Santa Claus. A man dressed in a red suit, his beard fake, but the smile he wore was real enough. His eyes crinkled at the corners, and he spoke to each of us with a kindness that felt like a gift of its own. I didn't question why Santa looked different than what I imagined. I was simply happy to see him, to believe for a moment in something good, something magical. The laughter that filled the room, the warmth of the fire, the smell of freshly baked cookies these were the things that made it feel like a real Christmas.

I remember the happiness I felt in those moments, the brief reprieve from the cold reality of the home. It was a fleeting thing, but in that small space, I was allowed to feel like a normal child again. No threats. No punishment. Just a day where I could hold my new toys, where I could laugh with the other children, where the fear that constantly gnawed at my insides was momentarily pushed aside.

One of the gifts I received that year was a small toy car, bright blue with silver racing stripes. It wasn't anything fancy, just a simple plastic toy, but to me, it was a treasure. I would spend hours running it along the edges of the windowsill, imagining it racing through far-off places, roads I might someday travel. At night, I kept it under my pillow, a tangible reminder that sometimes good things could happen. It became my talisman, a symbol of that moment when life had felt almost normal.

That memory stands in sharp contrast to everything else from that time, like a single flower growing through concrete. It is so vivid in my mind because it was so rare. So pure. It was one of the few times I could truly feel joy without it being tainted by the darkness around me. The memory of that Christmas stays with me to this day always a reminder that sometimes, even in the worst of places, even in the hardest of times, there can be a moment of light. I thank them for my Christmas miracle. It wasn't much, but it was everything to me. That brief spark of kindness, that brief acknowledgment of our humanity, is something I will carry with me for the rest of my life. Because sometimes, those small moments of unexpected joy are the ones that keep you going when everything else feels lost.

Chapter 27

Glencoe

The following summer, we went on a holiday to Glencoe. Everyone went together in a minibus, and I remember it well the hills towering all around us, the huge loch stretching out in front of me, as if it were an endless mirror to the sky. Across the water, there was the island where the graves of those who died in the Glencoe massacre lay. I thought about the history, the people who had suffered, and how their pain had been woven into the landscape, just like mine would be. It felt strange, like the land was holding the memories of its people memories that couldn't be erased. They got a local instructor to teach us how to canoe. The first time I held the paddle; I felt the thrill of control. The water was calm, and the instructor gave us the basic safety instructions. We were ready. The sun was shining brightly, warming my face. I could feel the burn on my red hair and pale skin, a constant reminder that the summer was fleeting, but this moment this moment felt like something real. This was the life. How could life not be like this every day, I wondered. It was a rare, peaceful day, a day I could almost forget everything that had come before it.

After dinner, we sat by a campfire in the woods. We told ghost stories, and the crackling flames made the shadows dance across the trees. The warmth of the fire was comforting, and for the first time in a long time, I felt like I was just a child again, surrounded by people who seemed safe. But the night brought no peace. My sleep was interrupted by a hand covering my mouth, silencing me before I could scream. I couldn't see who it was, but I knew. It was the bastard who had hurt me before. His presence was all too familiar. I could feel his weight on the bed, feel his hands as they pulled my pyjamas down. I tensed up as much as I could, trying to keep him away, but it didn't matter. The pain was unbearable, a cruel reminder of all that had been done to me before. He tried to force himself inside me, but I fought as much as I could. I wasn't going to let him take anything more from me, but he hurt me in the trying.

He stopped when I couldn't hold still anymore, and he left, but not before warning me: "If you tell anyone, I'll kill your brother." His words, cold and final, echoed in my mind as I lay there, paralysed with fear. I cried for the rest of the evening, my sobs silent against the pillow, praying that my brother would never wake up, that he would never know what had happened.

The next day, we climbed Ben Nevis. My legs ached with every step, my body bruised and broken from the night before. But I kept going. I had to. I couldn't let anyone see the weakness, the pain that was gnawing at me. I made it to the top, and as I stood there, looking out over the landscape, all I could think about was how badly I wanted to push him off the edge, how easy it would be to end it all in that moment. But as I made my way back down the mountain, the thought of what he could do to my brother kept me in check. I was too scared of what he might do. My brother was still so young, still so innocent, and I couldn't bear to think of what would happen if I acted on my anger. I didn't think I could trust the staff. In my mind, it felt like they were all complicit in what was happening. They instructed him to do it. They didn't, but that was how I felt. The feeling of being trapped, of having no one to turn to, haunted me.

The guilt, the shame, the anger all of it mixed in that moment. The sense of betrayal was overwhelming. The beautiful surroundings of Glencoe, the peacefulness of the loch, the calm of the hills none of it mattered. In that moment, all I could feel was the weight of what had been done to me, and the responsibility I felt for keeping my brother safe. I had to protect him, even if it meant carrying the burden alone.

Chapter 28

The Weight of Shame

Content Warning: *This chapter contains themes of self-blame, trauma, and emotional complexity.*

I have always felt shame about what happened, even now, as I write this, all these years later. The weight of it lingers, a constant companion that has never fully let me go. There are days when the shame is overwhelming when it feels like it's all my fault. Was it something about me that attracted him to me? Was it something I did? I have often wondered: Am I gay? Or it was just that I was vulnerable, and he knew how to exploit that vulnerability. These thoughts have tormented me for so long, and even now, I find myself grappling with them.

The truth is, I don't know. I don't have the answers. I've spent years questioning myself, searching for meaning in something that defies understanding. I've tried to make sense of it, tried to find some reason behind why this happened to me, but there is no clear answer, no logic to the madness of it all. It is something that was done to me, not something I asked for, not something I deserved. But the shame, that feeling of being tainted, of being somehow less than, is hard to shake off.

I remember a conversation I had with my wife a while ago. She asked me if I wanted to report what happened to the police, after all the scandals that had become known on TV, and I just froze. I don't know why I didn't want to report it. It was fear. Fear of reliving it, fear of how I might be seen. But I've always said something that I still believe with all my heart: No one is born evil. The person who did this to me, he wasn't born that way. He wasn't always a predator. I don't know what happened in his life, but somewhere along the way, something turned him into what he became.

I choose to believe that he was a victim too, in his own way. I don't know his story, and it's wrong to speculate, but I've always thought that there must have been something in his past that led him to hurt others. No one starts life wanting to hurt someone else.

That doesn't mean. I

Forgive him, or that I don't still feel the weight of what he did to me. But it does mean that, deep down, I hope he found a better life. I hope he found love, compassion, and the chance to heal, just like I have. I hope that, somehow, he was able to face whatever demons haunted him, the ones that drove him to hurt me and others.

It's a strange thing, holding onto that compassion while still carrying the pain. I can feel the hurt he caused me every day, and I'll never forget it. But I also know that holding onto anger or hate for him won't set me free. It's a burden, this understanding that he, too, was a product of whatever darkness shaped him. And that's the hardest part of all, realising that we're all shaped by our pasts, and sometimes, those pasts lead us down quite different paths. But as I sit here now, reflecting on all of it, I can't help but feel that I've found a better way, a way to heal, to move forward. My wife is part of that healing, her support and love guiding me through the darkest parts of myself. I don't have all the answers, and I may never fully understand why this happened. But I know that I am not to blame, and that understanding is something I had to find for myself. It's still a process, but it's a process that's slowly leading me out of the darkness and into something brighter.

I remember the day I went home; they came and got me. I had to say cheerio to the lads I left. I could see the look of hurt in their eyes. I didn't know what to say but we are going home to my brother he smiled a huge smile.

Chapter 29

The Adult Amnesia

When I came back from care, it was like stepping into a different world. My parents, the same ones whose tempers had filled our home with tension, had found God. They were saved, or so they said. And like a stone dropped into water, their salvation rippled through the whole house. We were all expected to find God too, to be saved, to join in on this new chapter of their lives as if everything that came before had simply been erased.

The house became a meeting place for Bible studies. Strangers sat in our living room, Bibles open on their laps, heads bowed in prayer. There were hymns and scripture readings, hands held, and eyes closed. It was like walking onto a stage where everyone else knew their lines, but I hadn't been given the script.

"It's a fresh start," my mother said, her voice light, too light.

"Were blessed to have a clean slate."

I didn't have the words for it then, but looking back, I called it 'adult amnesia.' They'd found a way to forget who they were, who we all had been, and the damage that lay in the wake of their old selves. It was as if their sins had been washed away, but the stains still lingered on us, the kids who had lived through it all.

I sat through the Bible studies, the prayers, the hallelujahs. I nodded along, memorised the verses, did what I had to do. But inside, I was a kettle on the boil. The idea that you could just say sorry to some invisible God and all would be forgiven boiled my piss. It felt too easy, too convenient. It felt like they were getting away with it.

"You need to forgive, Ian," they'd say, as if it was that simple. As if forgiveness were a box you ticked, a sin you could wipe clean with a prayer. But I couldn't forget. I couldn't close my eyes and pretend the past was gone just because they said it was.

One night, during yet another Bible study, I sat at the edge of the room, half in shadow. They were talking about redemption, about how God could take even the darkest of souls and bring them into the light. There was a story about a man who had been a drunk, who had hurt his family, but who had turned his life around after finding Christ. Everyone nodded, their faces soft with the glow of forgiveness. I bit my tongue so hard I tasted blood.

I wanted to say, "What about the people he hurt? What about the scars he left? Do they just go away because he is sorry now?" But I didn't. I knew how it would go. They'd say the past was in the past. They'd say I needed to move on. They'd say I needed to let God heal me, too. Instead, I slipped out of the room and into the cool night air. I walked until the voices faded, until I couldn't hear the prayers, until I felt like I was real again. It became my habit to walk away when the house filled with hymns and hallelujahs. I found my own places to pray, though I never thought of it like that. Under the sky, with no walls and no one telling me what I needed to feel, I could breathe. I could let the anger settle, let the hurt find its place. I could be honest with myself, even if no one else could be.

That was my truth. And it was enough.

Chapter 30

No Way Hosea

It was 1979, and I'd just come back out of care. I was in Primary Seven, the world around me shifting, and everything felt new and old all at once. My teacher that year was buzzing with excitement. The country was on the edge of something big, she said the first woman Prime Minister. Margaret Thatcher. She wanted us to understand how historic it was, to get us involved, to make us part of history. But I wasn't having it. Not a bit. "No way, Hosea,"

I told her, arms crossed, my jaw set. She looked at me, her face half bemusement, half curiosity.

"But why not?" she asked. She was one of those teachers who genuinely wanted to know, not just tell you what to think.

"My granddads would kill me if I did that," I said. I didn't really understand politics then, not the way adults did. But I knew enough. I knew what my grandfather's stood for, the stories they'd told me, the way they saw the world. And if they said, 'no Tories,' then that was good enough for me.

She let it go, or at least I thought she did. I figured she'd move on, find someone else to help her with her little school project. But at the end of term, she came to me with another idea.

"How about a speech?" she asked. "In front of the school, the parents the whole lot."

I blinked at her, my brain already screaming 'no' before my mouth caught up. "No."

She smiled, that patient teacher smile, and asked again. "Come on, you'd be great. You've got a good voice, and you're not shy."

"No."

This went on for days. Every time she asked, I said no. It became a game, but one I wasn't going to lose. I couldn't imagine anything worse than standing up there, all eyes on me. Besides, my parents wouldn't come anyway. They never did.

Then, one weekend, I was at my grandfathers. We were sitting in his kitchen, the smell of tea and pipe smoke filling the room. He looked at me over his cup, a sly grin on his face.

"So, I hear your no doing that speech," he said.

I nearly choked. I hadn't told anyone about it. "How do you know that?"

His grin widened. "Your teacher. She's the daughter of my Auld pal. We go way back. She said your just like me. Couldn't get me to go Tory either."

I sat there, my face burning. The bemused look on my teachers face made perfect sense now. She must've told him everything. The refusals, the stubborn 'no way Hosea,' the way Id dug my heels in. And here he was, proud as punch.

"Well," I said, trying to sound cool. "I'm not doing it." He laughed, the kind of laugh that started deep in his chest and rolled out. "Good on ye. Stand by what you believe. But next time, just tell her your grandad told you so. Save her the trouble of finding out."

We both laughed then, the sound filling the small kitchen, the kind of laughter that felt like a win. It was a strange moment, where defiance turned into connection. Where my stubbornness wasn't just a quirk, but a part of something bigger a link back to him, to the stories he had told, to the principles he lived by.

In the end, I never did the speech. My teacher didn't ask again, and I didn't offer. But every now and then, when I think about politics, about standing my ground, I remember that day. I remember my grandfather's laugh, the way he seemed to see right through me, and the pride in his voice when he said, "You're just like me."

And, of course, he still called me Speug. Always Speug.

Chapter 31

Freedom

When I moved back to Hamilton I stayed about 200 meters from my grandfather the gardener. He was now retired; he had five heart attacks in the last five years of his life. He would come down and see me often but often I would go up there. He kept the garden immaculate, but I would go to the shops and stuff for him. He used to send me to the bookies to put a line on for him. He always said I gave him luck. I'd give the line to the guy behind the counter, he knew my grandfather well. I was so glad I got to spend time with him before he died. He retired at 65 and he was dead at 66. He used to tell me war stories about how he was a commando, and he used to slit the throats of the Germans. He finally told me though he had been lying. He was a conscientious objector. Not because of morals or anything, he told me the story. He went to sign up in the navy with all his brothers, there were five of them. They had to go back and get their uniforms and start their basic training. Everything was fine. He was last in line; they gave all his brothers the navy uniform and gave my grandfather a commando uniform. This was a branch of the navy. He said you've made a mistake I am going to the navy and the sergeant said to him the commandos are the navy. My grandad said give me that uniform or you can go and fuck off. The sergeant was just as stubborn as my grandfather. He then said to my grandfather you'll wear that uniform or you will be going inside. Meaning prison. My grandfather said do what you want but I will not fight in that uniform. He ended up going to jail, he didn't get formally released till 1948. Most of the Nazis were out by then.

My dad was born in 1947, so I always used to joke with my grandfather, are you sure I'm your grandkid? He used to say of course I know, look at you. I was absolutely nothing like him. He did tell me though he used to get day release a lot in wartime, he played football for Blackburn Rovers. He had been dating my grandmother since 1945. This is an example of the man. On the night he and my grandmother got married, he told her then, now Emily, I am going to tell you this once and I will never ever tell you again. I love you and I worship the ground you walk on. But I am not the type of man to keep repeating myself. And he never ever told her again. But she knew.

Chapter 32

The Coal Bing

"Brother it is your turn." I shouted, pointing to the old car bonnet. He stood at the top of the coal Bing, his hands jammed into his pockets, breath puffing white in the frosty air. Aye, and break my neck? No chance! he called back, but there was a spark in his eye. He couldn't resist it. None of us could. You're just a big Jessie! my cousin taunted, his voice carrying through the cold. I'll show you how it's done! Before I could react, he charged past, throwing himself onto the bonnet with a wild yell. The metal scraped against the hard frost, coal crunching beneath it as he sped down the slope. His laughter turned into a scream as the bonnet twisted sideways, and he tumbled off, rolling into a patch of stinging nettles. Jesus! I ran down after him, my boots skidding. My brother followed, his reluctance forgotten. We reached him just as he sat up, his face red with cold and the sting of nettles. Instead of crying, he started to laugh a deep, uncontrollable laugh that made his whole-body shake.

You look like you've been attacked by a hedge! my brother snorted, and then he was laughing too. I couldn't help it. I joined in, the three of us tangled in the nettles, our hands raw and our sides aching. Docker leaves! I gasped between laughs. We need docker leaves!

We scrambled to find them, our fingers stiff and clumsy. The docker leaves were supposed to take the sting away, a kind of magic only kids believed in. We rubbed them over our skin, pretending it helped, still laughing at the sheer madness of it all.

The coal Bing had become more than just a playground it was a place where nothing else mattered. The cold, the frost, the ache in our hands it all faded away in the face of our laughter. Even when the coal Bing turned from play to necessity, when we were picking through the frostbitten dross for coal, those memories warmed us. We weren't just looking for coal. We were digging for a bit of summer, a

bit of the joy wed known on that old, rusting car bonnet. And in those moments, our thoughts felt as free as our laughter light, untethered by the weight of the world.
But summer didn't last forever. The next time we found ourselves on the coal Bing, it was out of necessity. The frost had bitten deep, turning the ground hard as stone. Our laughter had been replaced by silence, our fingers digging into the frozen dross, searching for lumps of coal to take home. Each scrape of stone against metal seemed to echo the dull scrape of our thoughts colder, sharper, more relentless.

"I can't feel my hands," my brother muttered, his breath a cloud in the chilly air. "Keep digging," I said, my own hands raw and bloody. The coal had turned sharp, each piece biting into our skin as we pulled at it, trying to break it free from the frost. The ground seemed to fight back, every shard of coal embedded in the earth as if it belonged to it, not us.

My cousin cursed, holding up his hand. Blood welled up from a fresh cut, dark against the coal dust on his skin. "Its bloody useless!" "Just a bit more," I urged. "Mum kill us if we go back empty-handed."

We kept at it; our fingers numb and our breath shallow. Every piece of coal felt like a victory, a small triumph against the cold. And through it all, the memories of summer kept us going the echoes of our laughter on the Bing, the feel of the swing over the River Avon, the warmth of the sun on our faces. My thoughts were like coal too sometimes buried deep and sharp-edged, but if I dug deep enough, I could find the warmth hidden within. "Remember the nettles?" my brother asked, a thin smile cracking his blue lips. I nodded. "Aye, and the docker leaves. Didn't help a bit." A chuckle escaped him, a quiet sound in the frozen air. "We were right daft." "Still are," my cousin added, his voice muffled by his scarf. "But well get through this."

And we did. Our hands were shredded, the frost biting into our bones, but we walked home with coal in our pockets and the memories of better days burning like a warm fire inside us. Even in the harshest winter, summer never truly left us. And neither did the thoughts of those warmer days embers that refused to die, no matter how cold the world became.

Chapter 33

Lady Hamilton's Estate

There was a world within the walls of Lady Hamilton's estate, a world where the past lingered in every stone and shadow. The gardens were a tangled maze of overgrown paths, where nature had started to reclaim its hold. Statues stood like silent sentinels, their features worn smooth by time and weather, faces frozen in expressions we used to mimic and mock. The statues were our friends, our enemies, our allies in the endless games we played.

The estate was a place where thoughts could roam as freely as our feet. It was as if the old stones absorbed our secrets, holding them in the cool earth beneath the ivy. When we whispered to the statues, we weren't just speaking to stone we were sending our thoughts into the past, hoping they might echo back someday.

"I bet that one comes to life at night," my brother whispered, pointing to a statue of a woman draped in ivy. Her stone eyes watched us, and for a moment, I almost believed him.

"Aye, and she probably eats little boys who tell fibs," I shot back, grinning. The truth was that the place had a magic to it.

Not the kind of magic you read about in books, but the kind that comes from being young, when the world is still full of mysteries.

The old air raid shelter was our fortress. Its concrete walls were damp, the air thick with the smell of earth and rust. The entrance was half-hidden by brambles, a secret door to a place where we could escape. Inside, we'd sit with our torches, the beams flickering against the walls, making shadows dance. It was a place for secrets and stories, for making plans that felt important, even if they were about which statue to climb next or how to sneak into the overgrown greenhouse without getting caught.

Our thoughts filled the space, layering over the old wartime echoes. The shelter became a vessel for them, a place where the weight of our minds could settle and rest. The damp walls absorbed them, turning the air thick with the unspoken our hopes, our fears, our childish imaginings. Even now, when I think of the estate, I don't just see the old stones and the overgrown garden. I see the possibilities, the magic, the way the past and the present seemed to blend in a place where anything felt possible. It was more than just a playground. It was a place where we could be whoever we wanted to be, where the statues watched over us like guardians of our childhood dreams.

Our thoughts, like the ivy, crept into every corner, wrapping the old stones in our own quiet truths.

Chapter 34

The Ruins of Chatelherault

Before it became the grand, restored hunting lodge it is today, Chatelherault was a ruin a shell of its former self, a place where history and nature had entwined. We discovered it long before the restoration, when the walls stood half-collapsed and the grounds were overgrown. It was the kind of place that called to us, a forbidden adventure waiting to happen.

The stone archways, weathered and crumbling, loomed like the bones of a giant beast, long dead but still lingering. Vines curled through cracks in the walls, creeping over the remnants of carved stone that once spoke of grandeur. The roof had caved in, leaving jagged edges where the sky bled through. It smelled of damp earth and old stone, a scent that seemed ancient, as if the place itself still breathed in the past.

We slipped through a gap in the iron fence, the old metal cold under our hands. Inside, the silence was thick, broken only by the wind whispering through empty window frames and the distant caw of crows. The floor was a graveyard of fallen beams, shattered bricks, and the debris of time. We picked our way through carefully, our footsteps muffled by moss that had crept over the flagstones like a green tide. In one of the larger rooms, we found something that sent a shiver down our spines a pentangle, drawn in what looked like old chalk, faint but still visible on the stone floor. At first, we laughed, dismissing it as some foolish prank, but there was an eerie weight to it, a feeling that prickled at the back of our necks. Who had drawn it? And why? The thought lingered even as we moved on, pushing deeper into the ruins.

There was a tree, massive and gnarled, growing right through the centre of the building as if it had claimed the place for itself. Its roots twisted through the stone, cracking it apart, while its branches reached toward the broken ceiling like skeletal fingers. We stood beneath it, staring up, feeling small in its shadow.

Even in its decay, there was something grand about Chatelherault, something untamed. It wasn't just a ruin it was a place that had refused to be forgotten. We felt that, even as kids. That sense that we were standing in the echo of something bigger than ourselves, something time had tried to bury but hadn't quite managed to kill.

The ruins seemed to hum with old thoughts remnants of the past that drifted through the open windows like whispers. It was as if every cracked stone held a memory, every fallen beam a fragment of someone's story. Our own thoughts mingled with them, turning the place into a tapestry of imagined histories and real hopes. I often wondered what the walls would say if they could speak. Would they whisper the secrets of those who had walked these halls before us? Or they would simply sigh, tired of holding the weight of so many stories.

There were moments when the place felt alive. The wind through the empty windows sounded like soft voices, just at the edge of hearing. Shadows seemed to shift, not with the movement of the sun, but with their own quiet intent. I sometimes caught myself staring into the empty rooms, as if expecting someone or something to stare back. My thoughts would spiral, creating stories that wove together ghosts and memories, turning each crack in the stone into a doorway to another world.

Even now, when I see the restored Chatelherault, polished and proper, I think of the old ruin. I think of the tree growing through the floor, the pentangle carved into the stone, and the feeling that we had stumbled upon something ancient and strange. It wasn't just a building back then it was a gateway to a world where anything felt possible, and where the line between reality and imagination blurred just.

enough to let the magic in. The thoughts we left there, like the old graffiti carved into the stone, still linger in the shadows, waiting to be heard. Sometimes, I imagine that if I stood very still and listened hard enough, I might hear them, my own childhood thoughts, echoing back to me through time.

Chapter 35

Cadzow Castle

Cadzow Castle sat on the edge of the Avon Gorge, a crumbling ruin that seemed to cling to the rocks by sheer will alone. The path to it wound through the woods, overgrown and half-lost to brambles, as if the forest itself wanted to swallow it up. Wed heard the stories the old castle where Mary, Queen of Scots, had once sought refuge. To us, it was just another adventure, another place to test our courage and see who among us would dare to go the furthest into the dark.

The castle was a place where our thoughts could unravel and reweave themselves into stories. Each shadowed archway became a portal; each echo a reminder that the past never truly leaves a place. As we moved through the ruins, I felt my thoughts drift between centuries, imagining knights and traitors, whispers of old alliances and the creak of ghostly Armour. The air was cool, damp with the smell of wet stone and earth, and every step seemed to echo, the sound swallowed by the stones but not entirely lost. One afternoon, when the sky was a washed-out Grey and the promise of rain hung heavy, we found an archway half buried in ivy. The green tendrils crawled over stone like fingers gripping tight, as if the castle itself were being pulled into the earth. We tugged and pulled at the ivy until a doorway emerged, a dark maw leading into the bowels of the ruin. "Go on, you first," one of us would say, and the rest of us would laugh, all bravado and grins. But beneath the laughter was a current of something else a mixture of fear and thrill that sat sharp on the back of the tongue. I went first that day, torch in hand, the light weak against the dark. The floor was uneven, stone giving way to earth, and roots twisted through the walls like veins. The others followed, our footsteps soft, our breath held. We found ourselves in a small chamber, the walls carved with old graffiti-initials, dates, symbols whose meanings we didn't know. We imagined secret meetings, prisoners scratching their names into the stone, a hope that someone, someday, would know they had been there.

Looking back, I realise how much I learned in those quiet, crumbling places. The castle taught me that history isn't just in books or museums it's in the air, the stones, the stories left behind. It was a place where I learned to listen, not just to the echoes of the past, but to the quiet within myself.

I began to understand that shadows weren't just the absence of light they were a reminder of what had been and what still lingered. That lesson stayed with me, shaping the way I looked at the world. I started to see the stories hidden beneath the surface of things, in the cracks and the quiet places.

Even now, when I think of Cadzow Castle, I remember that feeling. The gorge beneath, the castle above, and the sense that the shadows weren't just shadows. It was a place where history bled through, where the stones held secrets, and where a part of me still lingers, peering into the darkness and wondering what might stare back. The castle taught me to sit with the unknown, to embrace it rather than fear it. In a way, it prepared me for life is shadows the ones that creep in during the quiet moments, asking you to face what you'd rather ignore.

Years later, when life threw its darkest shadows my way, I found myself thinking back to that ivy-covered doorway, to the way my torchlight had barely pushed back the dark. I realised that sometimes, you must step into the shadows to find what's hidden there. You must investigate the darkness and trust that, whatever you find, you'll be able to face it. Cadzow Castle had been my first lesson in that a lesson in courage, not the kind that comes with chest-thumping bravado, but the quiet, steady kind. The kind that carries you through when the world around you feels like its crumbling, and all you can do is hold on, like those stones, and refuse to let go.

Chapter 36
The Blue Waters

Blue Waters was a place of legend. The old quarry, filled with water so blue it seemed otherworldly, sat hidden off Strathaven Road. It was the kind of place you had to know about where the trees leaned in close and the world seemed to hush as you approached. The waters strange, mineral blue shimmered in the sun, a quiet invitation that we could never resist.

We went there every chance we got. Summers were spent jumping from the rocks, the icy water swallowing us whole, the shock of it leaving us breathless and laughing. The place had a magic to it, as if the water held echoes of the past, rippling with secrets.

But the Blue Waters had a darker side too. The stories swirled around us, whispered in the twilight when the air grew cold and the wind tugged at our jackets. There was the tale of the ghost train the one that had derailed and plunged into the quarry, its iron bones swallowed by the blue depths. Some said you could still hear it on quiet nights, the rattle of wheels on rusted tracks, the mournful whistle that seemed to rise from the water itself.

One summer night, we decided to camp there. It was a spur-of-the-moment thing, a dare that none of us wanted to back down from. We brought a couple of old blankets, a packet of crisps, and a torch whose battery was half-dead before the sun had even set. As darkness fell, the Blue Waters turned black, the surface still and waiting.

"Tell us a story," my cousin said, his voice low, the kind of tone you use when you want to sound brave but don't quite manage it.

"Aye, but make it a scary one," my brother added, his face lit from below by the torch, his features twisted into a mock snarl.

I thought for a moment, the sounds of the night pressing in. "Have you heard about the train?" I asked. The others went quiet, their faces turned to me, the torchlight throwing long shadows.

"They say it was a goods train, back in the day," I began. "One of those old steam engines, chugging along in the dark. The driver never saw the landslide rocks tumbled down onto the tracks, and the whole train went over, straight into the quarry. It sank fast, the steam hissing, the water closing over it. They say everyone on board went with it."

"But it was just a train, right?" my cousin interrupted, his voice a little too high. "No passengers?"

I hesitated, drawing it out. "That's what they say. But old Tommy that bloke who used to drink outside the chippy he said he saw more. Said he had been a boy when it happened, that he watched the train go under. He swore blind he could see faces pressed against the windows, hands banging against the glass as it slipped under."

"Shut up," my brother whispered, but I could see the fear in his eyes, the way he kept glancing at the water.

"And on quiet nights," I continued, "if you sit real still, you can hear it. The train, still running its route, trapped under the water. The rattle of the wheels, the echo of that last whistle. Sometimes, if the moons right, they say you can see the lights of the carriages, moving just beneath the surface."

Silence fell over us, the kind that feels like a weight. The torch flickered, the shadows danced, and somewhere out in the darkness, a twig snapped. My cousin yelped, his crisps spilling over the blanket, and the rest of us jumped up, laughing, the tension breaking like a spell.

"You're all a bunch of fannies," I said, but my voice shook, and none of us sat back down. The Blue Waters felt different then, the surface still but hiding something. We didn't see the ghost train that night, but as we made our way home, the stories came with us, trailing behind like mist, lingering at the edges of our dreams.

Chapter 37

The Tunnel at the Nature Trail

At the top of the nature trail in Hamilton stood the tunnel. It was a massive, gaping mouth cut into the hillside, its stone arch swallowing the path whole. Wed passed it a hundred times before, usually in daylight, when the sun turned the stone Grey and the inside seemed more like a cool escape than a threat. But this time was different. It was late, and the light was already fading, the shadows growing long and thick.

"Are you sure about this?" my brother asked, his voice a mixture of bravado and doubt. He clutched the torch, its yellow beam thin and wavering.

"Aye, it'll be fine," I said, though my own nerves buzzed under my skin. "It's just a tunnel."

The air turned cool as we stepped inside, the temperature dropping so fast it felt like a breath on the back of your neck. Our footsteps echoed, a steady crunch of gravel underfoot. The tunnel seemed to stretch on forever, a straight shot into darkness. The torchlight barely reached the walls, revealing only damp stone and the occasional rusted pipe. "Do you think it goes all the way through?" my cousin asked, his voice bouncing off the walls.

"Maybe," I said, though I had no idea. It was the not knowing that made it exciting. Every step took us further from the safety of daylight, the entrance shrinking behind us until it was just a pinprick of light.

About halfway through, the torch died. One moment we were surrounded by its dull yellow glow, the next, the world went black. My brother smacked it against his palm, the plastic case cracking but giving no light. "Bloody things knackered," he muttered.

"What now?" my cousins voice was a whisper, the kind that made your skin prickle.

"We keep going," I said, trying to keep my own fear out of my voice. "It's straight. Just put your hand on the wall and follow it."

We shuffled forward, our hands brushing the cold, wet stone. The air felt thick, and every sound seemed too loud the rasp of our breath, the scuff of our shoes, the drip of water somewhere deep in the tunnel. My imagination started to play tricks on me. I could hear things soft shuffles, distant whispers, the scrape of metal against stone. Or it wasn't my imagination. I really could hear the rats, their tiny claws scratching through the darkness. "Did you hear that?" someone asked, and the panic in their voice was like a match to dry kindling.

"Its rats!" my brother yelled, and that was it. We ran. We ran like the devil himself was at our backs, tripping over each other, falling to our knees, scraping hands against stone, but always getting back up. Our breath came in sharp, painful gasps, our feet pounding out a desperate rhythm. The tunnel seemed to close in around us, the darkness growing thicker, pressing against us.

I could barely see. My hands slid over the damp wall, and every time I thought I'd lost it, panic spiked sharp and hot through my chest. I fell, my knees cracking against the stone, pain jolting up my legs, but I scrambled up again, my only thought to keep going, to get out.

Finally, the exit loomed ahead, a patch of pale Grey against the black. We burst out into the open air, collapsing into a heap on the wet grass, still laughing, and swearing and catching our breath. The sky stretched wide above us, and the world seemed too big, too bright after the suffocating dark of the tunnel.

We didn't go back. Not for a long time. Even now, when I think of that tunnel, I can feel it the cold, the darkness, the sense of something just behind me, breathing down my neck. I don't know if there were really rats or if it was just our fear, but it doesn't matter. In that moment, it was real enough to make us run.

Chapter 38

The Loch Lomond Adventure

It started as a brilliant idea. We were going to cycle from Hamilton to Loch Lomond a gang of us with nothing but our bikes, backpacks, and the bright hope of a grand adventure. Wed camp under the stars, cook over a fire, and tell stories until we fell asleep to the sounds of the great outdoors. In our heads, it was perfect. It was anything but. We set off early, the morning air still cool, our bikes rattling as we peddled through the familiar streets. The journey took us right through the middle of Glasgow, weaving along the banks of the Clyde. We were a ragtag bunch, our backpacks bulging, tent poles strapped to handlebars, and pots and pans clanking with every bump. It was just as we hit a busy road that disaster struck. My backpack, already straining under the weight of our 'camping gear,' gave up. The zip tore open and out tumbled our precious cargo. Pots and pans hit the tarmac, bouncing

and clattering in all directions. It was like a kitchen explosion in the middle of traffic. Cars honked, drivers swerved, and
one particularly unlucky frying pan took a hit, spinning under a bus.

"You've killed it!" my brother shouted, as if the pan had been a family pet.

"Leave it!" I called back, grabbing what I could and shoving it into my already bursting pockets. The rest was lost to the road, flattened, and scraped, a trail of metal breadcrumbs marking our path through the city.

By the time we reached Loch Lomond, the weather had turned. What had started as a light drizzle had grown into a full-on downpour. The ground was already soaked, puddles spreading underfoot. We tried to pitch the tent, our fingers numb with cold, the fabric heavy with water. The tent poles had a mind of their own, bending and snapping, refusing to take shape.

"Just hold that end," I snapped, but the wind whipped my words away, and my cousin let go, sending the half-pitched tent into a spin.

The fire was no better. Every match we struck fizzled out, the wood refusing to catch. We huddled together, our jackets pulled tight, a useless pile of damp kindling at our feet. "What's for dinner then?" someone asked, their voice hopeful.

"Fish fingers and beans," I said, holding up a soggy packet. The fire was a lost cause, and we were too wet and tired to try anything else. We ate them cold, chewing on half-frozen fish fingers and scooping beans straight from the tin. It was a meal of pure desperation.

When the rain finally eased, we crawled into the half-collapsed tent. It leaked, of course, and none of us slept. Every rustle outside was a bear, every drop of rain a reminder of just how far from home we were.

We gave up the next morning, damp, dirty, and defeated. The ride back was quieter, the bikes heavy, our spirits low. But by the time we rolled into Hamilton, the whole trip had turned into a joke. We told the story over and over, each time laughing harder, the disaster of Loch Lomond becoming one of our favourite tales to tell.

Looking back, I wouldn't change it. It was a lesson, not just in how not to camp, but in how sometimes the best stories come from the worst plans. And that sometimes, cold fish fingers and beans under a leaking tent can be as much an adventure as anything else.

Chapter 39

Scrumping

When I was a wee lad, there was a house by the railway that belonged to a man named Mr Stepek. His place was well-known in the town, not just for the old house itself but for the orchard he had in the back garden. His trees were heavy with fruit apples and, more importantly, those perfect, golden pears. I swear, they were the best pears you'd ever tasted, the kind where the juice would run down your chin before you even realised.

One crisp autumn day, a few of us decided to go scrumping. We didn't think of it as stealing, not really. It was more of an adventure, a sort of rite of passage. You'd hear whispers from the older kids about how sweet the fruit was, and the stories of daring escapes only added to the thrill. To us, it felt like we were only borrowing the fruit before the birds could get it.

We crept around the side of the house, hearts thumping in our chests. There was a low fence, nothing that could keep out a determined boy. We slipped over it with all the stealth we could muster. The orchard stretched out before us, trees bowing under the weight of their harvest. The pears dangled there, swaying gently in the breeze, practically begging to be plucked.

We scaled the nearest tree, our hands and knees scraping against the rough bark. I can still remember the feel of the branch under my feet, the smell of damp leaves, and the first bite into a warm pear. It was heaven until it wasn't. A low, guttural sound cut through the quiet, like the rumble of thunder. I froze, pear halfway to my mouth. The other lads looked at me, wide-eyed, each of us wondering if we had really heard it. Then the noise came again, louder, and angrier.

Geese. Bloody geese.

Mr Stepek, in his infinite wisdom, had a flock of them acting as living, hissing alarm bells. They rounded the corner of the house, necks outstretched, eyes fixed on us like we were the worst kind of thieves. Which, I suppose, we were.

Their honking wasn't just noise it was a full-on assault. Each honk seemed to vibrate in my chest, a deep and throaty sound that promised nothing but trouble. The hissing was worse, like steam escaping a kettle, sharp and relentless. The geese moved like a wave, their white bodies surging forward, wings half-raised like they were preparing for flight or a fight.

The noise was relentless, a chorus of fury. The honks seemed to echo off every tree and wall, a barrage of sound that made it impossible to think. They hissed with a venomous intensity, their long necks bobbing as they moved, beaks opening and closing as if they were casting some kind of avian curse. Their wings flared out, each beat a whip crack against the air, and the ground seemed to shake under the thunder of their webbed feet.

We dropped from the tree in a scramble of elbows and knees. I felt the sting of a nettle patch as I hit the ground, but fear numbed the pain. We bolted for the fence, geese snapping at our heels. Their beaks clacked with every stride, and their wings thrashed against the air, whipping it into a frenzy. I could hear the hiss and the beat of wings behind me, the sound of the others shouting. My feet barely touched the ground.

When we finally made it over the fence, I collapsed onto the pavement, chest heaving, the pear still clutched in my hand. The geese stopped at the fence, honking their victory as we lay there, too scared to laugh, too relieved to move. That was the last time I ever went scrumping, but to this day, every time I see a goose, I feel that same jolt of terror.

The geese had won that battle, but at least Id gotten my pear.

Chapter 40

Learning the Hard Way

Five years. That's how long the house remained filled with the sound of Bible studies, hymns, and prayers. Five years of sitting at the edge of the room while strangers thanked God for their blessings and my parents tried to rewrite the past through faith. I learned to keep my head down, to stay out of the way, to make myself small enough that God would forget to test me for a while.

At school, things weren't much easier. When I started high school, I could hardly write. I'd spent so much of my early years bouncing from one place to another that reading and writing had never really taken root. I was behind before Id even begun, and the first few weeks wanted to try to run through mud. The other kids seemed to glide through it, their pens dancing across the page while mine scratched and stuttered, the letters awkward and unsure.

I never studied. Not once. It wasn't that I didn't want to learn it was just that, by the time I got home, the last thing I wanted was more words, more lessons, more expectations. My brain felt full of static, a constant hum that blocked out anything useful. I'd sit at my desk, the workbook open, and all I'd see were the gaps between the lines, the empty spaces where the answers should be.

"You need to apply yourself," teachers would say, their voices the same mix of exasperation and pity. "You're not living up to your potential."

I didn't know what my potential was. I wasn't sure I had any. But I knew how to survive. I knew how to listen just enough to get by, to pick up the pieces of information that floated past, and string them together into something that looked like learning.

Slowly, it started to click. Words made sense. Sentences came together. I began to understand not just what the teachers were saying but why they were saying it. It felt like finding a door in a wall I hadn't even realised was there. The first time I drafted an essay that didn't come back covered in red pen, I stared at it for ages, afraid I'd made a mistake, that it wasn't real.

I got a couple of O-Grades in the end. Not top marks, not the kind of grades that opened doors to grand futures, but they were mine. Id earned them without studying, without anyone pushing me, without help. I walked out of school with those pieces of paper in my hand, feeling like Id won something not against anyone else, but against the idea that I wasn't enough.

Looking back, I think That's what made them so important. It wasn't about passing. It was about proving to myself that I could do it. That I could pull something out of the chaos and make it mine. It was a small victory, but it felt like the world.

Chapter 41

Young Love

When I was 17, I fell in love for the first time. Not the sort of crush that fades with the changing seasons, but the kind that knocks you sideways and fills your head with dreams. She was everything to me, the kind of girl who could make the world seem brighter just by being in it. I was daftly, madly in love, the way only a teenager can be completely, without caution.

She stood by me through everything. When I left for the nursing role down south, she was my lifeline. We spoke all the time, the kind of long phone calls that made the cord stretch across the room, voices soft and filled with plans. I'd sit in my tiny room, books piled up around me, my head full of anatomy and care plans, and hearing her voice made it all feel worthwhile.

Life was brilliant. I was studying, learning more than I ever thought I could. I was partying too, finding that balance between being responsible and being young. There were late nights, both at the hospital and at the pubs, a blur of laughter and fresh faces. But no matter where I was or what I was doing, she was always there, a constant thread running through the chaos.

We were making it work. The distance didn't matter, not when everything else felt so solid. She believed in me, even when I didn't believe in myself. And for the first time, I felt like I was building a life that wasn't defined by where I'd come from, but by where I was going. I had love, a purpose, and a future thing I'd never thought I'd find, all wrapped up in the possibility of what lay ahead.

Chapter 42

The First Step

I couldn't wait to leave home. Even though things seemed better, they were only better in the way a half-healed wound feels less painful, but still raw if you pressed too hard. My parents had found God, found forgiveness, found fresh faces to show to the world. But the old ways lingered under the surface, slipping through the cracks every now and then, sharp and cutting. The cruelty was different, less about survival and more about control, but it was still there. A reminder that people don't really change they just learn to hide what they are.

When I was about 19, I saw an advert for a student nurse role. It felt like a door cracking open, a glimpse of something beyond the four walls of my childhood. I already had a job at an old folk's home, doing personal care and helping wherever I could. It wasn't glamorous work, but I liked it. There was a quiet satisfaction in looking after people, in being useful, in seeing the difference you could make just by being there.

The advert said you didn't need qualifications you could get in through an entrance exam. That was my chance. I applied, half expecting nothing to come of it. But a letter arrived, inviting me to sit the exam. It was the first time Id felt real hope in a long time, the kind that sits warm in your chest and makes the world look a little less Grey. On the day of the exam, I turned up at a building that felt far too big, the ceilings high and the corridors echoing. I sat in a room with a dozen other hopefuls, the kind of silence where even breathing felt too loud. The exam papers sat in front of us, and for a moment, all I could think about was how many times Id failed before Id even started. But this was different. This was my way out. I read each question twice, careful, deliberate. I let the pen move slowly, shaping my thoughts into words, the letters steady on the page. It wasn't perfect, but it was honest. It was me. When I finished, I handed the paper over, my hands cold, my stomach twisted. The lady marking it didn't make me wait. She sat there, her pen scratching against the paper, her face unreadable. I felt every tick and every pause, my heart climbing into my throat. I had to do an essay on the north south divide. They came back to me and said Ian your essay is not up to par would you like to do it on something else. I remembered a topic from school and the who, what, when, why, and where. I rewrote an essay about the seaside.

Finally, she looked up. "You've passed," she said, her voice bright. "Do you know how rare that is? Only one in twelve passes on the first try. This is brilliant."

I stood there, the words soaking in slowly, like water on dry ground. One in twelve. And I was the one. I wanted to laugh, to cry, to run out into the street and shout it to the world. Instead, I just nodded, my mouth too dry to speak, my hands fisted tight to keep them from shaking. Coming home, I felt different lighter I had dared to dream. The world seemed full of doors waiting to be opened. I thought about the old folks I looked after, the way a small kindness could brighten their day, the way their stories wrapped around me like blankets. I thought about my parents, about the house full of prayers and platitudes, and how I was finally stepping out of it.

It wasn't just a job. It was a first step. A chance to build something new, to find my own way, to become someone more than the boy who had slipped through the cracks. as I walked, back from the train station. The chilly air biting at my cheeks, I felt something I hadn't felt in a long time. I felt free.

Chapter 43

My Grand Mother

It was my first time back home since heading down south for my nursing course I was stationed in Essex, Bishop Stortford< Harlow and Epping. I was upstairs, lying in the bath, letting the warm water wash away the long journey and the weight of being back under my parents' roof. I had plans that night going out with my girlfriend, escaping the house, even if just for a while. I was in that half-awake state, the steam rising, the world muffled by water and ceramic.

Then I heard it. Shouting from downstairs. My mothers voice, sharp and relentless. My grandmother had moved in with my parents after my grandfather died. She had suffered a stroke about six months before, and it had stolen all her words. The only two she had left were fucking bastard. I remember thinking, Leave her alone. She is frail. She's had enough.

The shouting grew louder, a wave of noise crashing through the house. Then, cutting through it all, came a scream my name, twisted and raw. "Ian!"

I moved before I knew what I was doing, water sloshing over the bath, the towel barely clinging to me as I tore down the stairs. My grandmother was in the room downstairs, lying on a bed that had become her world since the stroke. She had collapsed, her body crumpled, the life draining from her face even as I reached her. Training kicked in. I checked her airway, listened for breath, felt for a pulse. Nothing. My hands moved on their own, lifting her gently to the floor. The carpet pressed into my knees as I started CPR, my palms pressing down on her chest, the rhythm of life and death counting through my head.

My mother was there, still screaming, her voice a blade against my concentration. I looked up, my hands never stopping, and I saw her face a mask of fear and chaos, but not action. Useless.

"Make yourself fucking useful," I snapped, my voice a sharp edge. "Phone an ambulance."

Her mouth opened and closed, the words tangled up inside her, but she moved. The call was made, the minutes dragged out, and still, I kept going. Breath and press, breath, and press. Each cycle a prayer, each compression a plea. I did everything they had taught me at college; every step drilled into me until it was muscle memory.

But this wasn't a training dummy. This wasn't a scenario or a test. This was my grandmother. The woman who had loved me, who had stood by me, who had been one of the few constants in a world that seemed to shift under my feet. And I couldn't save her.

I never got her heart started. I felt the life slip through my fingers, a whisper against the chaos. The room seemed to shrink, the walls pressing in, the air too thick. I wanted to scream, to shake my mother, to make sense of the storm of emotions crashing through me. Instead, I kept going, long past the point where hope had left the room.

I've never shaken the feeling that my mother killed her. Not with her hands, but with her words, with the anger that filled every corner of the house. I know, logically, that it was just my own feelings coming through, the old hurts and the raw edges of a childhood spent on the defensive. But the thought lingers, a shadow that stretches across that day. What I do know is this: I did everything I could. I used every ounce of training, every drop of love, and every bit of strength I had. And when it wasn't enough, it left a scar. One that still aches, one that still makes me pause when I think of her, when I think of the last words she ever said, those two, raw and real. "Fucking bastard."It's strange, the things that stay with you. It's not the sound of her voice, the way her hand felt in mine, the coolness of her skin against my lips as I kissed her goodbye. When I think of my gran, I can just see her dead face and lifeless eyes and memories of my air coming back out of her lungs having no effect. I still feel her sometimes, in the quiet moments, in the space between thoughts. And I hope, wherever she is, she has found peace. Because I haven't. Not yet.

Chapter 44

Broken Twice

Going back to college after my grandmother died was like dragging myself through a fog. I was still traumatised, still carrying the weight of what had happened, but I managed. I went through the motions, attending classes, showing up to shifts, and putting one foot in front of the other. My training helped me compartmentalise, to push my feelings down and keep moving. It was survival, plain and simple. My fiancée was my anchor. Wed gotten engaged, and despite everything, we believed we could make it work. We had six months until the wedding, and the thought of it was the light at the end of an exceptionally long tunnel. She stood by me through it all, a reminder that there was still good in the world. I was in love, truly, and for the first time, I felt like my life was on the right track.

When I went home to see her, my heart was full of plans and hope. But when I arrived, there were police cars outside her door. My soon-to-be brother-in-law ran out, his face pale, his movements frantic. He grabbed me, his fingers biting into my arms, and told me what no one should ever have to hear.

She was gone. Sudden Arrhythmic Death Syndrome, they called it. She had gone to bed and never woken up. Just like that, the future I had been holding onto unravelled, the threads slipping through my fingers, leaving nothing but empty air. I never seen her again even her casket was closed as they had done a full postmortem examination. For years later I seen her everywhere the mind and heart still scanning for her.

My heart broke for the second time. The kind of break that you can hear, a crack that echoes through every bone, every thought, every dream. I moved through the days like a ghost, my body present, but my mind somewhere else somewhere darker, somewhere I couldn't reach. I made it through the funeral, my hands numb, my face a mask. People offered their condolences, their words falling against me like rain on stone. I couldn't absorb any of it. Couldn't find warmth or comfort in the hymns, in the prayers, in the well-meaning hugs. I felt nothing, and then I felt everything, and it was too much.

I couldn't face it on my own. The emptiness, the silence, the weight of what had been taken from me. I thought I'd found freedom. I thought my life stretched ahead of me, wide and open, and that I'd be my own captain. I thought I'd found someone to share it all with. I was wrong.

In the end, I didn't want to hurt any more. I wanted to slip away, to find that same quiet she had, the peace that came with closing your eyes and not waking up. I tried to take my own life. I won't go into the details there's no need. What matters is that I was found by luck. A neighbour, a stranger, a stroke of fate. They got me to the hospital, pumped my stomach, and pulled me back from the edge. I remember waking up, the lights too bright, the beeping of machines, the antiseptic smell of the ward. I thought I was free, that I had found a way out, but life had other plans. I was still here, still breathing, still carrying the weight of it all. And in that moment, I knew that if I was going to stay, I had to find a way to live with it. To keep going, even when the path seemed too hard, too long, too dark. And so, I did. Not because I was strong, but because I had no other choice. I had lost everything, but I still had life.

And, just maybe, that was enough to start again.

Chapter 45

How Much Can a Person Take?

Life wasn't finished with me. Not by a long shot. I thought that by going back to college; by throwing myself into my nursing course, I could find a way forward. Id survived the worst of it, I thought I had. Id pulled myself back from the edge, held onto the threads of my life, and set my sights on a future that still made sense. But life had other plans. They called me into a room. The kind of room where the walls are too white, the chairs too small, and the air too still. There were two of them professionals, the kind who talked with soft voices and careful words. They told me I couldn't continue with the nursing course. I wasn't 'strong enough' now. 'Emotional resilience' they called it, as if it were something you could measure, something you could fix with a plaster and a pat on the back.

I felt like the ground had been pulled out from under me. How much more could a person take? How many times could I get back up when life kept knocking me down? I had already lost so much my grandmother, my fiancée, my future as I had imagined it. Now, the one thing I had left, the one thread of purpose I had been clinging to, was gone. I left the college, the echoes of their words following me down the halls. I packed up what little I had, found a flat, and moved in. The place was small, barely more than a room with a bed and a window, but it was mine. I sat on the edge of that bed, the silence pressing down on me, and I felt the weight of it all. The loss, the grief, the anger it settled on my shoulders, a blanket of stone. For six months after I came home, I drank and drank and drank some more the alcohol didn't take away the pain. I was suicidal deeply I would lie on the sofa I could never sleep in the bed again. I heard a key in the latch, and she came in and lifted my head off the sofa. And gently stroked my hair telling me she was safe and happy with her beloved grandmother. She told me to move on start taking care of myself and live for her as well as myself. She said I will always be watching keep your head up and smile. Ironically, she knew absolutely nothing of my previous life I didn't want to tell her. I was too ashamed of who I was, I just was not worthy. Most people who know me don't know, it came out sometimes, on a professional level. some people Know parts the only person that knows it all is my wife. it took years before I let it out the bag, she is right. Julie says I held in the crazy for years then it spilled out. too right it scares everyone away. So back to getting back to normal well as normal I can be.

I needed a job. Something to keep me moving, to keep the days from swallowing me whole. I found work as a waiter. It was a strange shift from caring for people in hospital beds to carrying plates to their tables. From studying anatomy to memorizing the specials board. But it was work, and it kept me going. The routine of it, the back-and-forth of a busy shift, the way the hours blurred together until I could almost forget the ache in my chest.

I became good at it. I learned how to smile, how to move through a crowded room without really being there. I poured drinks, served meals, cleared plates. I heard snatches of conversation bits of laughter, arguments, the hum of normal lives being lived all around me. I stayed quiet, a ghost in a waiter's uniform, floating through their world without ever touching it.

It wasn't the life I had planned. It wasn't even close. But it was life. And for the time being, that was enough. One step at a time, one shift at a time, I kept going. Because what else could I do?

Chapter 46

Detonators

We were always finding things around the railway tracks. The tracks ran like a scar through our town, cutting through the backyards and under bridges, a path to nowhere and everywhere. It was a place where kids like us could disappear for hours, the clang of distant trains a reminder that the world was bigger than the grey streets we called home One afternoon, we were walking the tracks when Mick spotted it. A small, round metal disc, dull and weathered but unmistakably out of place among the gravel and rusted rails. We all crowded around it, peering at the thing like it might suddenly come to life.
"What is it?" I asked, keeping my hands tucked firmly in my pockets.
"It's a detonator," said Mick, with all the authority of an eleven-year-old who had once heard his uncle talk about the railway. "You know, for trains."

None of us really knew what a detonator did, not properly. Wed heard stories, of course how railway workers used the metal discs to signal trains, to let them know when danger was ahead. They were meant to go off with a bang.
if a train rolled over them, a warning shot to the driver. But no one had ever said what would happen if you hit one with a hammer.
Naturally, we had to find out.
Mick ran home, and in no time, he was back with his dad's old hammer. It was a heavy thing, with a wooden handle worn smooth by years of real work. He handed it to me, and the weight of it made me feel a bit braver, like I was holding a sword instead of a tool.
"Go on then," he urged, a grin spreading across his face. "Give it a whack."
I didn't want to. I really didn't. But there were four pairs of eyes on me, and the last thing I wanted was to look like a coward. So, I crouched down, the cold metal of the detonator glinting up at me. I could see my own warped reflection in it, my face stretched and strange.
I raised the hammer, my arm feeling suddenly heavy. Time seemed to slow, and all I could hear was the thud of my own heartbeat, the rustle of the wind in the long grass.
Then I brought the hammer down.

The bang was like a gunshot. No, louder. It was as if the earth itself had cracked open. My ears rang with it; the world reduced to a high-pitched whine. Gravel shot out in all directions, stinging my shins and biting into my cheeks. I fell back, the hammer slipping from my hand, my fingers numb and tingling.

Mick screamed. We all did. There was no thought, only movement, as we scrambled to our feet and ran. We tore down the tracks, blind and deaf, our feet slamming against the wooden sleepers. My legs felt like lead, my chest tight with fear and the sting of grit in my throat.

We didn't stop until we reached the old bridge, where the tracks disappeared into darkness. We huddled together, our backs against the cold, damp stone. I couldn't hear anything but that relentless ringing, the echo of the bang still bouncing around inside my skull.

"Do you think they heard it?" one of the lads asked, his voice thin and far away.

"Of course they did," I muttered, rubbing at my ears. "The whole town must've heard it."

We sat there for what felt like hours, waiting for sirens, for angry men with uniforms and questions we couldn't answer. But nothing came. Eventually, the ringing faded, and the real world slipped back into focus. Birds sang. The tracks lay quiet and empty, as if nothing had happened. When we finally crept back, the detonator was gone. Someone had taken it, or it had been blown to bits. All that was left was the hammer, half-buried in the gravel, the metal head dented, and the handle splintered. I picked it up, feeling the rough edge of the wood under my thumb, and slipped it into my bag. I wasn't sure why. It was a reminder, or a trophy. Or I just didn't want to leave anything behind that could tie us to the bang.

That night, I lay in bed, the boom of the detonator replaying behind my closed eyes. Every time I blinked, I saw the flash of light, the scatter of gravel. I couldn't help but think of all the things that could have gone wrong, of fingers and eyes and the kind of injuries that didn't heal. We never talked about it again. Not properly. When it came up, it was always with a laugh, a joke about the time we almost blew ourselves up. But there was always that edge, a shadow in the corners of our grins. We had played with something we didn't understand, and for once, wed gotten away with it.

But every now and then, when I walk by the railway and hear the distant rumble of a train, I feel that echo in my chest. The ghost of a bang. And I know that some things, some sounds, never really go away.

Chapter 47

Cheap Cider

The first time I got drunk, as a teenager, I need to differentiate from when I wasn't in the care home as I was drunk their loads. Started both smoking and drinking in the home. But this was at home, it was in the park. I was thirteen, fourteen the exact age is fuzzy, like most things from back then. We were a ragtag bunch, a mix of schoolmates and kids from the estate, all of us looking for something to do, or something to forget. The park was our place. It had a swing set with rusted chains and a roundabout that creaked with every turn, a sound that could have been laughter or a warning.

It started with a bottle of cheap cider. The kind with a garish label, sold in plastic bottles that crinkled when you held them too tight. We passed it around in a tight circle, each of us taking a swig, our faces twisting at the sour bite.

I'd never tasted anything like it, sharp and sickly sweet, a tang that clung to the back of my throat. But I kept drinking. We all did. There was a sense of camaraderie in it, a shared rebellion, the kind that only kids who feel caged can understand.

It didn't take long before the world started to sway. The trees moved in a way that made me dizzy, their branches waving like the slow-motion arms of drowning men. I giggled at nothing, at everything. The ground seemed to soften under my feet, and I ended up sitting, then lying on the damp grass. My head spun, and the sky twisted with it, stars swirling like sugar in tea.

Mick was there, of course. He always was. He had a cigarette in his hand, the smoke curling up into the night. He passed it to me, and I took a drag, coughing so hard my eyes watered. I didn't like it, but I didn't want to say so. The need to belong was stronger than the burn in my lungs. From there, it didn't take long for other things to find their way into our circle. The older lads would show up, the ones who had already left school, or never bothered much with it to begin with. They brought more than cider. There were roll-ups that didn't smell like tobacco, and when you took a drag, the world went soft around the edges. I remember the first time I felt it, the slow melt of everything hard and sharp. It was like sinking into a warm bath after a week in the cold.

It felt good, and then it didn't. Because after the weed, there was glue. Little plastic bags with a smear of something pale inside. It was strange how quickly it happened; how easy it was to go from cider to smoke to solvent. We sat under the slide in the park, inhaling deeply, the smell of chemicals filling our heads until we were somewhere else entirely. The world became a smudge, a blurry painting with no edges, no rules.

I remember the way my heart raced, the thud of it in my chest like a drum beat just out of time. I thought I might die, and part of me didn't care. Part of me welcomed it, the way you might welcome the end of a bad dream. But then the rush would fade, and the world would come back, colder, and harder than before. I would see Micks face, his eyes glassy and far away, and I knew he was feeling it too that mix of escape and regret.

Back then, getting your hands on a bottle of Strongbow cider wasn't hard, even if you were only twelve. It wasn't the strongest drink, but it was strong enough for us. The shopkeepers didn't ask questions, and we didn't offer answers.

We'd pool our change, send in the bravest of us, and they'd come out clutching the bottle like it was treasure. It felt like a secret, a small rebellion, a step closer to being grown-up though the reality of it was far from what we imagined adulthood to be.

We were just kids. But back then, childhood felt like something to get through, not something to enjoy. The park was our refuge and our ruin, a place where we could disappear from the eyes of the world, if only for a little while. We told ourselves it was just fun, just messing about, but there was a sadness in it, a shadow that crept in around the edges. It wasn't just the cider, the smoke, or the glue it was us, trying to find something that felt real in a world that didn't.

Looking back, I'm not sure when the fun stopped and the danger started. It was a slow slide; a gradual erosion of whatever innocence we might have had left. But I do remember that first night, lying on the grass, the world spinning above me, and thinking that, just maybe, I'd found a way to stop feeling afraid. If only for a moment.

Chapter 48

Smoke and Swagger

I was about fourteen when my parents caught me smoking. The way they reacted, you'd think I'd been caught sacrificing goats in the back garden. They sat me down, stern faces on, and told me smoking was a filthy habit that would put me in an early grave. I nodded along, the obedient son, but behind my eyes, I could already see the lecture stretching on, endless and pointless.

Then, in their infinite wisdom, they devised a plan. "Right," my dad said. "If you want to smoke, you'll smoke. Margaret, go to the shop and get him twenty."

I thought they were joking. I mean, I'd heard of reverse psychology, but this was something else. My sister, looking half bewildered and half delighted to be part of the drama, trotted off to the shop and returned with a fresh pack of twenty cigarettes. My mum opened the packet, handed me a cigarette, and lit it.

"Go on then, big man," she said, her voice dripping with a mix of sarcasm and something that might have been hope.

Hope that Id crumble, cough up a lung, and swear off smoking for life.

I took a drag, slow and deliberate. I didn't cough. I didn't splutter. I just sat there, blowing smoke rings while my parents watched, their plan already slipping through their fingers. Inside, though, I was feeling sick as a pig. My head spun like a record on the wrong speed, and my stomach churned with every drag. I thought if I could just hold out a bit longer, I'd win.

"Another," my dad said, his voice harder this time. "Keep going."

And so, it went. One cigarette after another. My hands were shaking, but I masked it by flicking ash with a practiced ease I'd seen older lads use. Each drag burned, and I could feel the smoke clawing its way down my throat. The world around me started to blur at the edges, and my heart thudded unevenly in my chest. But my face? Cool as a cucumber.

At one point, I thought I might pass out. The room tipped sideways, and I had to blink hard to keep my focus. Every instinct screamed at me to stop, but I couldn't. Not now. My parents wanted to break me, and if I gave in, they'd never let me forget it.

Finally, after what felt like hours, the cigarettes were gone. My parents sat opposite me, arms crossed, lips pressed into thin lines. They looked more uncomfortable than I felt. The smoke hung thick in the room, like a curtain drawn on some ridiculous play.

"How do you feel now, big man?" my dad asked, his voice full of a sneer. They were expecting me to break, to wretch, to admit defeat.

I leaned back in my chair, exhaled a final plume of smoke, and said, "I feel like another twenty."

There was silence. I had won, but the victory tasted like ash. They never tried that tactic again, and I suppose, in a way, neither did I. The taste of smoke lingered, but it wasn't from the cigarettes it was the smouldering embers of whatever bond we might have had.

When they left the room, I barely made it to the toilet. I threw up everything my pride, my stubbornness, and what felt like my soul. I knelt on the cold bathroom floor, head against the porcelain, and laughed between heaves. It was a mad, choking sound, but it was mine.

Chapter 49

Psychobilly

As I hit my late teenage years, I started to grow into my own identity. I had my hair cut in a psychobilly style massive quiff, about eight inches off my forehead. My brother always said it looked like a traffic cone on my head. I wore white bleached jeans, dyed by my own hand, always with a pinstripe jacket in the summer and a long Crombie coat in the winter. I'd get my gear from charity shops, the best place to find treasures if you knew how to look. I thought I had style, a swagger that couldn't be touched. In my mind, I was untouchable, a walking statement. I was a young lad trying to make sense of where I fit into a world that seemed more interested in breaking me than building me up.

It was the 1980s, a time when fashion was as much about rebellion as it was about expression. Everywhere I looked, people were carving out their identities with safety pins, denim, and enough hairspray to take out the ozone layer.

But for me, it wasn't about following a trend. It was about telling the world I was here, I existed, and I had a voice, even if it was just a whisper among the chaos.

I remember walking into charity shops, the musty smell of old fabric and forgotten lives hanging in the air. I'd spend hours sifting through racks, fingers brushing against tweed and leather, looking for something that called out to me. I became an expert at spotting a diamond in the rough a tailored jacket, a waistcoat with just the right amount of wear, a pair of shoes that had danced through decades. Those shops were a treasure trove, a time machine, and they became my sanctuary. In those aisles, I could be whoever I wanted to be.

One of my best finds was a battered leather jacket. It had seen better days scratches across the arms, a small tear on the collar but to me, it was perfect. I imagined the stories it held, the lives it had touched. When I wore it, I felt like I was part of something bigger, a lineage of those who had lived on the edges, the outsiders. It became my Armour, a second skin that told the world I was more than what they saw on the surface.

Of course, not everyone saw my style as a declaration of independence. My mother looked at me as if Id turned up in a clown suit. What's that on your head? shed ask, her voice dripping with disdain. Id shrug it off, but her words would settle on me like a cold drizzle, unwelcome and hard to shake. My dad barely noticed. He was lost in his own world, a place I could never reach. Sometimes I wondered if he even saw me at all.

School wasn't much better. I was a target, a beacon for bullies who couldn't resist taking a shot at the lad with the hair you could hang a coat on. They'd sneer, throw words like knives, but I learned to dodge. My sharp tongue became my shield, humour my weapon. I discovered that if I could get a laugh, I could diffuse the tension, turn their jabs into a joke I was in on. It was a skill Id keep for life, a way to survive when the world pressed in too close.

But there were moments of magic too. I'd walk into town, the soles of my charity shop brogues tapping out a rhythm on the pavement, and for a while, I was part of the world. People would nod, some would smile, a few would stare, but it was all fuel. It kept me going, kept me believing that one day, I'd find my place, my people, my peace.

Looking back, I realise that style was more than just clothes and haircuts. It was a survival strategy, a way of claiming my space in a world that often felt too narrow, too Grey. My psychobilly quiff might not have lasted, but the confidence it gave me did. I might have been a young lad trying to make sense of it all, but in those moments, I was more an echo of who I would become, a storm child finding his way.

Chapter 50

Snakeskin Boots

The television hummed softly in the corner of the room, its glow casting long shadows over the worn-out sofa and the carpet with a burn mark no one remembered the origin of. I was half-watching, half-thinking about nothing at all, when the familiar plunking of a guitar pulled me out of my daze. There he was. George Michael, in all his denim-clad glory, leaning against a jukebox, tapping those damn boots against the side of it. His hair was perfect, his smile sharp, and the camera adored him. But all I saw were my own boots my beautiful snakeskin boots with Cuban heels and metal toe and heel pieces reduced to a pop culture prop. Something twisted inside me. Those boots had been mine, my little rebellion, my quiet act of defiance against the mundane. They weren't a fashion statement or a music video accessory. They were for strutting, for standing a bit taller, for feeling like the world couldn't quite touch me.

Now, thanks to George Michael, they were nothing more than a trend.

I could've just put them away, shoved them to the back of the wardrobe until the fad passed. But no. I needed something more definitive. I needed to make a statement, even if it was just to the universe and the patch of garden behind my flat.

I grabbed the boots, feeling the cool metal under my fingers, the smoothness of the leather. They'd taken me to gigs, through rainy streets, and out of places I should never have been. They'd made the satisfying clack against pavement that said, 'I'm here.'

I stepped outside, the air damp and the sky a moody Grey. There was a patch of dirt where the grass had long since given up the fight. Perfect. I stood the boots up, arranging them as if some invisible ghost still wore them. Then I found an old rag, doused it in lighter fluid, and stuffed it into one of the boots.

It took only a flick of the lighter. Flames whooshed up, curling and snapping, turning snakeskin to ash. The fire danced, and for a moment, it almost felt like freedom. An effigy to Faith No More. A promise to myself that I wouldn't let the world take anything else from me without a fight. When the flames died down, there was nothing left but charred leather and metal. I stood there a bit longer, the smell of smoke and burnt offering heavy in the air. And somewhere, beneath the smirk, I felt a little bit lighter.

Those boots were gone, but they'd gone my way not. George Michael's. And that, at least, was something.

Chapter 51

The Zoot Suit.

The zoot suit wasn't just clothing it was an attitude. The moment I slid my arms into those oversized shoulder pads and buttoned up the square-cut jacket, I felt the shift. The world outside might stay the same, but I wouldn't. Not while I wore it. It was more than fabric; it was a passport to reinvention. I didn't just walk down the street; I swaggered. I owned the ground beneath my feet, my boots striking pavement with a rhythm all their own.

The suit had weight to it, both physical and metaphorical. The thick fabric swung around my legs, each step a reminder that I was choosing to stand out. The metal toe and heel pieces on my boots clicked with every step, a sharp, metallic echo that turned heads but left me feeling untouchable. I liked the way people noticed not because I craved attention, but because, for once, I could control why they looked. I was no longer the invisible kid, the one who slipped through the cracks and barely left a mark. The suit made sure of that.

But I reserved it for special trips, to Glasgow. The city had a pulse that beat to its own rhythm, and I felt more at home there among the bustle and the unspoken agreement that everyone was just doing their own thing. No sideways glances or snide comments just a crowd of people walking their own lines, each thread part of the tapestry but never tangled. I could get away with it in Glasgow, slipping into the city's current and letting it take me wherever it led. There was a freedom in those streets. Id weave through the crowds, the suits wide shoulders creating a buffer zone, a space where I could just be. Id stops in record shops, flicking through vinyl covers, pretending I had the money to buy them. Id wander into vintage clothing stores, looking for anything with that same feeling the sense of stepping into a story, of borrowing someone else past for a while. Sometimes, I'd find a cafe with a window seat, nursing a coffee until it went cold. I'd watch people pass by their lives intersecting with mine for just a heartbeat. I'd make up stories about them a man in a grey overcoat was a spy, a woman in a red scarf had just walked away from a life she no longer wanted. It was a game, but it was also more than that. It was a reminder that the world was full of stories, and mine didn't have to follow the script I'd been handed. The zoot suit became part of those stories. It was my way of writing myself into the world, a character of my own making. And when I finally took it off, hanging it back up in the wardrobe, I always felt a twinge of loss, as if I was shedding more than just clothes. But I knew it would be waiting for me, ready to transform me again when the city called my name.

Chapter 52

The Journey In

The train rides into the city were their own little rituals. Sitting in those worn, patterned seats, I'd see my reflection in the window, half-shadowed by the passing scenery. The zoot suit always looked sharp against the drab greys and browns of the everyday world. I liked how it jarred with everything around me, like a bright shard of glass in a field of pebbles. Sometimes Id catch people looking, but not for long. I wore the suit like Armour, and most folks knew better than to pick a fight with someone wearing something so bold.

When the train rolled into Glasgow Central, it was like stepping into a different world. The architecture, the echoes of voices, the smell of fried food and damp stone it was a sensory assault, but a welcome one. The city was a canvas, and I had every intention of leaving my mark.

Nighttime in Glasgow was when the zoot suit truly came alive. The lights hit the fabric exactly right, casting strange, angular shadows. Id slip into the clubs or pubs, not necessarily to drink but to soak up the atmosphere. The music, the hum of conversation, the laughter it all washed over me, and I could just be. No past, no future, just the beat of the moment.

Sometimes Id dance, the suit swaying with me, drawing eyes but never questions. There was a freedom in it, a rhythm that only existed under neon lights. The zoot suit was more than clothes it was Armour, a disguise, and a declaration all rolled into one. It was my rebellion, my way of saying, 'I am here, and I am more than what you see.' I met people, shared stories, laughed with strangers whose names I never learned. There was always a moment when the music hit exactly right, and the world outside the club faded away. It was a suspended reality, a place where nothing could touch me. I could be anyone I wanted, and no one would ever know.

The suit became a talking point, an icebreaker, a mask, and a mirror all at once. It let me be whoever I wanted to be mysterious, bold, untethered. I could feel the energy of the room, the unspoken stories, the dreams clinging to the edges of reality. It was intoxicating, a buzz that no drink could match.

Some nights, I'd find myself in conversations that bordered on the absurd. A man once told me he was a secret agent, his breath heavy with whisky. I thought he was just another knob till he showed me the gun. He had it strapped to his body like in the American TV shows. Another night, a woman in a sequined dress gave me her number. I was sitting with a crowd of guys, and I saw her come over. I tossed the number away wasn't interested. One of the guys I was with picked it up. I hope it worked out for him. Glasgow had a pulse at night, a thrum that seemed to synchronise with my own. The streets were never empty, not really. There were always shadows moving, echoes of lives I'd never know. Id slip out of a club just as the night started to tilt toward morning, the air cool against my skin. The suit, now rumpled and tired, felt like a second skin, holding the nights secrets in its creases.

The city itself became a part of the ritual. The stone buildings, dark and heavy, the wet pavements that shimmered under the streetlights, the graffiti that changed every week but always seemed to say the same thing' We were here.

We mattered.'

When the night ended and I walked back to the train station, the suit still held that energy, like a talisman against the mundane. The chilly air would bite, a reminder that the night couldn't last forever. But for those few hours, I was invincible, a part of something bigger than myself, part of the city's heartbeat. It was in those moments that I found a sense of belonging, a fleeting connection with the world around me, even if I remained a stranger within it.

It wasn't always magic, though. There were quiet nights when the clubs felt empty despite the crowds. When the music was too loud, the lights too bright, and the zoot suit felt like a costume I couldn't take off. On those nights, I'd leave early, finding solace in the walk home, the rhythm of my steps replacing the lost beat of the club.

Looking back, those nights taught me more than I realised. About people, about masks, about how sometimes the bravest thing you can do is smile through the pain.

Chapter 53

The Morning After

Coming back to the real world after a night in Glasgow was always a bit of a shock. The suit would be carefully hung up, the fabric still holding the scents and echoes of the night before. I'd put on my usual clothes, the Armour packed away, but the feeling lingered. Reinvention wasn't about what you wore. It was a mindset, a choice. And that choice to be bold, to be different, to not give a toss about what anyone thought stayed with me long after the suit had been put away.

After a long night, my friends and I would end up in Dunkin Doughnuts, sipping on cheap coffee and taking over a booth like squatters who paid rent in conversation. We'd sit there until the first buses started to roll, watching the city shift from night owls to early risers.

The coffee was always terrible, a bitter, watery brew that left a faint chemical aftertaste. It wasn't about the coffee, though it was about the ritual. The heat of the cup against my hands, the comforting hum of the fluorescent lights, the way the world outside the window seemed to blur as night tipped into morning.

People watching was the absolute best. Everyone's life played out in little snippets a couple arguing over something petty, a lone soul lost in thought, groups of giggling teens who hadn't yet learned to be self-conscious. It was a window into a thousand untold stories, and I never got tired of it.

There was the old man who always sat by the window, his hands curled around a steaming cup, staring out as if he could see all the way back to his youth. Once, a woman sat opposite him, her hands waving as she spoke. He never looked at her, just nodded occasionally, his eyes never leaving the glass. I imagined he was listening to a ghost; someone he had lost long ago. The woman never came back, and he returned to being just another fixture of the dawn.

The early-morning workers were next the ones with grease under their nails and the weight of the day already on their shoulders. They ate fast, heads down, their conversations short and practical. I could tell who was new by the way they still looked up when the door opened, as if hoping for a reason to walk back out.

Sometimes, we'd catch sight of someone still carrying the night on their skin smudged eyeliner, clothes crumpled and creased, the faint scent of cigarettes and sweat trailing behind them. They were like ghosts, too, slipping between the world of the awake and the world of the dreaming. You could see it in their eyes, the dazed expression of someone not sure where they were meant to be.

Every so often, a drama would unfold. A slammed door, a heated whisper, someone storming off into the chilly morning. Those were the best moments. You could spend hours dissecting them, turning over every gesture and glance like an archaeologist brushing dust off old bones. The buses would start their slow crawl, hissing to a stop outside the window. One by one, the night creatures would shuffle away, replaced by parents with tired eyes and kids in school uniforms, backpacks too big for their small frames. The city's rhythm would change, a new beat to carry it through the day. Wed stay until we couldn't anymore, until the coffee turned cold and the staff started to clean up around us. Eventually, wed step back into the world, the dawn light sharp and clear, feeling like wed just lived a dozen different lives without leaving our booth. Those mornings were magic, a little secret world before reality set in.

Chapter 54

A New Chapter

Life ticked along. The days blurred into each other, a steady rhythm of work and sleep, with little in between. I moved through it, not really living, just existing. The joy had gone out of things, and the world seemed to have lost its colour. There were challenges more than I care to go into, but I got through them. Id learned how to survive, even if that meant just getting from one day to the next. Five years went by. I wasn't a waiter anymore. Id found work at a huge dairy in Glasgow, and for the first time in a long time, I felt settled. The work was hard, but it was honest. I liked the routine, the smell of the fresh milk, the way the machines rumbled and hummed through the day. I liked the guys I worked with too. They were a good bunch down to-earth, the kind who would take the piss out of you one minute and stand by you the next. It was a simple kind of camaraderie, but it mattered.

I started dating a girl and she fell pregnant. I don't know why but I couldn't let her in. I couldn't trust her. And the love just wasn't there, I remember the day the child, was born like yesterday. Her mum though, used to keep throwing me out, saying I was hiding stuff from her. She was right, I was but I knew if I told her any, of this she would use it against me. One day she through me out and I wouldn't go back. I kept supporting the child though. And keeping paying my way. I never thought though keep receipts. I was sofa surfing at the time and was crashing with people for a couple of days at a time. Time ticked by still working 6 nights a week in the dairy.

And then, everything changed. I went down to Dumfries for a night out. I wasn't expecting anything. Just a few pints, a bit of a laugh, a chance to shake off the dust of the week. But that night, I met her the woman who would become Mrs Hughes. She had a smile that lit up the room, a laugh that made everything else fade away. I don't remember what I said, only that I couldn't stop talking to her. She made me feel seen, like I wasn't just a shadow, moving through my own life.

We talked until the bar closed, and then we kept talking I walked her home and said my goodbye. There was something easy between us, a connection that felt natural, unforced. She wasn't just listening to mesh understood. She got the jokes, but more than that, she got me. It had been a long time since Id felt that. Since Id allowed myself to.

We met up the next day, arranged a date for the following weekend. I was still working in Glasgow and for the first three months till I got a job in Dumfries I was travelling up and down daily. It wasn't a dream; it wasn't just the beer talking. And for the first time in a long time, I felt hope bright, sharp, and new.

It was the start of a new chapter. One I hadn't seen coming, but one I was ready to write. One day at a time, one step forward, the world beginning to fill with colour again. The receipts came back to haunt me. When my ex found out about Julie she approached the case. 9 full months of 20 percent earnings. Still, we got through it together.

Chapter 55

Full Circle

Julie and I got on great from the start. We moved in together, got a house, and made it our own. It wasn't just a place to live it was home. We got married, surrounded by friends and family, and started building a life together. A real life, with laughter and plans and the kind of quiet comfort Id spent my whole life looking for. We had three wonderful children. Each of them a mix of the best and worst of us, but always their own people. I made it my mission to embarrass them at every opportunity terrible dad jokes, bad dancing, the whole lot. They'd roll their eyes and groan, but there was always a smile tucked in there somewhere. And watching them grow into the incredible people they are today, I've never felt prouder. We got married the year later big family wedding even my mother and father were there. Yeah, I invited them. They had no power over me now. However, they were still the same people my son was playing with his grandfather I was watching really watching. My son who was about four or five hit him too hard much like I had done twenty off years before. And up came the hand and he hit my son on the face that was it bubble burst. Get out my house and don't come back. After that I kept my visits to a minimum I was lucky I stayed seventy miles away. With the advent of social media and the internet I could keep in touch with who I wanted. My parents didn't like it but hey ho my kids are number one priority.

The house is quiet now. They've all moved on, finding their own paths, building their own lives. Julie and I are alone in the house, and while it feels a bit empty sometimes, theirs a peace to it too. We have earned this quiet, this chance to just be. There's no more chaos, no more battles to fight. Just the two of us, sitting side by side, the world a little softer around the edges.

Every now and then, I catch myself listening for the sounds of kids running through the halls, the slam of doors, the hum of everyday life. But instead, There's the gentle creak of the house settling, the rustle of pages as Julie reads, the steady tick of the clock. And I think to myself this is what it feels like to have made it. To have come full circle. And I wouldn't change a thing.

I returned to college and earned a Higher National Diploma in Photography and even opened a shop. The walls of the shop were lined with my photograph's snapshots of quiet moments, landscapes, and candid portraits that captured life as it was. I had hoped to bring a bit of light to a shadowy world, but opening a business during a recession wasn't the smartest move. The footfall was slow, the rent unforgiving, and eventually, I had to close. I stood at the door on the last day, the 'For Sale' sign tapping against the glass, and felt a sharp pang of failure.

But failure has always been a fertile ground for growth. I eventually returned to my passion for social care. At 48, I enrolled in university, a decision that both terrified and thrilled me. When I applied to study social work, the rejection stung. You don't have a qualification in mathematics, they said, as if numbers could measure compassion. I shifted course and pursued a master's in health and social policy. Because I did well in the HNC, I was allowed to skip the first year, but it wasn't the free pass it seemed. The academic world had its own language; one I had never been taught. I struggled with basic writing skills commas, sentence structure, the ebb and flow of an argument. I'd sit at the kitchen table, pen tapping against my teeth, and rewrite the same paragraph ten times, each draft a small step closer to finding my voice. In university, I sometimes felt dismissed. The lecturers spoke of policies and frameworks as if they existed in a vacuum. What qualifies you to speak on this matter? a lecturer asked me once; his tone edged with scepticism. I lived it, I responded, feeling a hot coil of anger in my chest. I had experienced the very policies we were discussing the failures, the gaps, the coldness of institutions. I wasn't drawing from theory but from memory, from scars and survival. Despite my qualifications and experience, the world of work often ignored me. I attended interview after interview, my suit a bit more worn each time, my hope a bit more threadbare. Impressive insights, one interviewer said, but were looking for someone with more traditional experience. It was a blow that reverberated deep within me. Traditional experience. As if the life I had lived, the hurdles I had leapt, counted for nothing.

Chapter 56

Missing Photographs

It started off with conversations on how I didn't seem to have a history. I didn't have any photographs. The absence of a photograph might seem like a small thing to most people, a lost snapshot, a forgotten keepsake. But for me, the fact that there is no record of my childhood, no photo of a young, wide-eyed boy standing in line at school with a hesitant smile, speaks volumes. It's a reminder of the quiet ways in which I was overlooked, not just by the world but by those who should have seen me first. I had seen all Julies photographs; her mum got them all out and relished in embarrassing her daughter.

Every year, when the school photographer came, I would stand in front of the backdrop, my shirt as clean as I could manage, my hair combed by my own careful hands. I would smile, as instructed, not knowing that the image would never find its way home. I remember the excitement in the classroom when the photos arrived, the kids comparing their prints, showing them off like tiny pieces of validation. I would watch, my hands empty, wondering what my own photo looked like how I looked to the world. I never got those photographs I didn't go holidays. Every time I left care nothing came with me. I am sure I must have had some taken at the home or at Blackwood even. I can remember getting a photograph with me wearing a jumper with an Indian on the front when I was a youngster, I didn't have it no one did, so it must have seemed like I just dropped out of the air.

The truth was that my parents never bought them. The few pounds needed to purchase a memory, a captured moment of childhood, were always too much. It was the money, or it was something else something about me not being worth that small expense. I learned early on not to ask why, to pretend it didn't matter. But it did. The absence of those photos became another echo of all the little things that were missing.

There was one year, when I was about nine, that I remember particularly well. The photographer had caught me exactly right the light through the classroom window casting a soft glow. My friend Colin had his photo in hand, a glossy rectangle that showed him grinning, his front teeth newly grown in, his uniform neatly pressed. Have you got yours, Ian? he asked, holding it out to show me. His pride was palpable, the kind of pride that came from seeing yourself the way others see you important, worth capturing. No, not yet, I lied, my voice light, even as my chest tightened. Next week.

I don't think Colin noticed the crack in my voice. He just shrugged and tucked the photo back into its envelope, the conversation moving on. But I stood there, my hands empty, the sting of it settling deep inside me.

It was strange throughout the years, looking at old photographs of other families, their memories held safe in glossy paper and wooden frames, while hiding that I had none to show. When conversations turned to childhoods, to 'Look how young I was!' and 'You can really see the family resemblance,' I learned to smile and nod, a practiced motion. My own history a blank page where photos should have been.

Even now, when my own children bring their school photos home, I find myself staring at them a little longer than I should. I see their joy, their pride, and I make sure every picture is displayed, treasured. I know what it feels like to be unseen, and

Chapter 57

The First Real Photograph

It wasn't until I was married that I finally saw a picture of myself that felt real. My wife and I stood together, arms wrapped around each other, our smiles genuine and unforced. The photo was taken by a photographer, staged, and planned, and when I saw it, I felt something shift inside me. I was seen truly seen not just as a face in the background or a name on a list but as a person worth capturing. Looking at that photo, I felt a kind of healing I hadn't expected. It was as if, in that captured moment, the boy who had stood empty-handed in the school corridor was finally holding something real. There I was, in a moment of happiness, frozen in time not just existing, but living. I began to take photos of everything.

Our early days of marriage, the quiet moments at home, the first smiles of our children. I wanted to make sure that nothing was lost, that every fleeting moment was captured and held onto. I was trying to make up for the lost years, for all the empty frames of my childhood. I wanted to surround myself with evidence that I existed, that I mattered, that the life I had built was real. One day, my daughter asked me, Dad, do you have any photos of when you were little? I hesitated. No, love. There aren't any. She looked at me, her young eyes full of confusion. Why not? I forced a smile, reaching out to brush a stray hair from her face. No one thought to take any. Her frown deepened, and she reached for my hand. Well, we've got lots now. I'll take your picture if you want.

Her words, so simple and pure, brought a lump to my throat. I'd like that, I whispered, my voice catching. And she did lift her mum's phone and snapping a photo of me sitting at the kitchen table, a cup of tea in hand, the afternoon light spilling through the window. It was an ordinary moment, but to me, it was everything.

Looking through the albums now, I see the story of my life unfolding in those photos. The boy who was once invisible has become the man who keeps every photograph, every memory, every piece of evidence that love and life are real. It is a quiet rebellion against the pasta way of saying, I am here. I was always here.

Chapter 58

Scars Into Stars

Eventually, I found work with children in care. But working in social care proved far more difficult than I had anticipated. It was too close to the knuckle. Every time I saw a scared face, I saw myself. Every time I was required to participate in a hold restraint, it felt alien like I was betraying the child within me. I was far too much on the kids' side, and that made the job impossible. Writing this now, it feels strange to admit that, but the truth is, I needed to be a step away from the coal face.

I couldn't properly back up the staff, and I couldn't properly back up the children. I was stuck in the middle, my empathy a double-edged sword. But I was kind, and I hope the children I looked after having fond memories of our time together. I found another way to connect with them through stories and adventures. I would weave tales of haunted houses, take them to explore the ruins, and bring the past to life in a way that wasn't frightening but instead filled with curiosity and imagination. I taught them how to canoe, how to build fires safely, how to make smores and roast marshmallows over open flames.

My dog would join us on walks, his wagging tails a reminder that not all things bite. My goal was simple: to turn an ordinary day into an amazing one. Whether through storytelling, outdoor activities, or simply being present, I wanted to offer them what I had always longed for moments of joy and the sense that someone cared. On their last day, I shared my story with them. I'd sit with them, a cup of tea between us, the soft hum of the boiler in the background. I sat where your sitting, I'd tell them. I know that same fear. I wanted them to see that the future wasn't just a dark tunnel but a path with twists and turns, yes, but also light.

One young man, his hands shoved deep into his pockets, asked, you made it through university? There was disbelief there, a shield against hope. I smiled. I did more than make it through. I turned my scars into stars. The room was quiet; the kind of silence that lets words settle. I wanted to show them that university was for people like us, people who had lived through hardship and come out stronger. Your dreams aren't behind you, I'd say. They've just taken a different shape.

And as I walked away, hearing the door click shut behind me, I knew that my story wasn't just mine any more it was theirs too, a seed of possibility planted in the rough soil of their lives.

Chapter 59

The Invisible Battle

Mental health is often like a storm that no one else can see. It rages quietly, a tempest within, where the winds of anxiety and the weight of depression twist through the mind like an unrelenting gale. My struggles with mental health began early, though I didn't have the words for it at the time. How could I when survival itself was the focus of each day?

There were days when getting out of bed felt like scaling a mountain. When the weight of the world pressed down on my chest, and the air felt too thin to breathe. When the echoes of my childhood the fear, the violence, the uncertainty seemed to whisper that I was still that frightened boy, powerless and small.

Living with complex PTSD and EUPD (Emotionally Unstable Personality Disorder) is like navigating a maze of shadows. The past often feels like a heavy cloak draped over my shoulders, tugging me back into moments I'd rather forget. Triggers can appear out of nowhere smell, a sound, a fleeting thought yanking me from the present and into old fears. My mind sometimes races, filled with self-doubt and the echo of old criticisms. I've had days when I felt disconnected from myself, as if I were watching my life from the outside, struggling to ground myself in the moment. EUPD adds another layer of complexity. Emotions can swing sharply, from overwhelming sadness to anger, sometimes without an obvious reason. It's a constant battle to find stability, to keep the world from feeling like its shifting under my feet. Relationships, too, can be challenging. I've often found myself questioning the intentions of those around me, wary of being hurt again. It's a balancing act, finding the courage to trust, to let others in while keeping the protective walls I built as a child from closing me off completely.

During one of my darkest days, a friend said something that has stayed with me: "Ian, the sky's still blue, and water is still wet."

It was such a simple truth, but it anchored me. When everything felt chaotic, those words reminded me that the world still held beauty, constancy, and small comforts, even when my mind couldn't see them.

But I wasn't alone. The more I opened, the more I realised that everyone carries their own storms. I found solace in small things: the warmth of the sun on my face, the steady rhythm of my breathing, the quiet strength of those who stood by me. I learned to reach out, to ask for help, to sit with the difficult feelings rather than running from them. Therapy became a lifeline, a safe harbour in the storm. Talking to someone who could guide me through the dark, help me untangle the knots of my past, gave me a sense of control I hadn't known before. Medication, too, became a tool not a weakness, but a support, like a rope to hold onto when the waves threatened to pull me under.

Through it all, I discovered that healing wasn't about erasing the past but learning to live with it. The storm might always be there on the horizon, but I had built a stronger shelter. I had learned to weather it. And on the days when the skies were clear, I found joy. Not the loud, fleeting kind, but a quiet, lasting peace that felt like sunlight after a long, dark winter.

Chapter 60

Thanks, and Reflections

As I look back on everything that has shaped me, the path I've walked, the struggles I've faced, and the triumphs I've achieved. I am filled with gratitude. I've come so far from the storm child, from the boy who didn't know where his life was headed. I've learned that life isn't about perfection. It's about survival, growth, and learning how to build something better out of the broken pieces of the past. The most important lesson I've learned is that our beginnings don't define us. They don't dictate how the story ends. The cycle of trauma I feared could be mine forever, the one I thought would consume me, was broken by a single, simple choice: to create a different life for my children. To give them the stability and love I never had. That is my real victory, the true success of my journey.

I want to thank my siblings, who shared in this journey with me. Their strength, their support, has been a constant reminder of why I fought so hard for a better life. I also want to thank all my grandparents, but especially my grandfathers. Their love, their lessons, and their quiet wisdom helped shape me into who I am today. I wish I had told them what they meant to me, but I carry their love in my heart.

I owe a special thanks to my foster parents. They gave me hope when I didn't think I could hope any more. In their care, I found a sense of security, a belief that maybe life could be different, better. They treated me like their own, and that made all the difference.

And then, there was the gentleman who owned the greenhouse. His kindness, though quiet and simple, gave me a solace I still feel to this day. In that space, among the tomatoes and the smell of the plants, I found a moment of peace midst the chaos. It became a refuge, a place where I could breathe, where I could remember what it was like to feel safe. I didn't know his name, but I will always remember his kindness.

This journey hasn't been easy, but it has brought me to a place where I can see the value in all that Ice been through. The pain, the losses, and the lesson they have shaped me.

And in looking back, I'm able to see the gifts that came from the darkest moments. Strength, resilience, hope these are the things Ice built from the rubble.

For all those who have been part of my story, for all the people who have shown me love and kindness, I am deeply grateful. You gave me the strength to move forward when I couldn't see a way ahead. You helped me believe in something better.

Chapter 61

Hopes and Dreams

To all the other storm children out there: This too will pass. You may not see the way forward now, but the storm will eventually break, and you will emerge stronger. Hold on, for better days are ahead. I have started writing, as well as this book, I'm in the process of drafting a three-novel epic fantasy. Two are already completed. I'm writing the other at the same time I am writing this. It's to keep me busy and to keep the demons away. They are in no way like this. This is about getting the memories out of my head and onto paper. It has been quite cathartic, and I'm enjoying the process. But by no means do I feel like an author. In the next couple of years, I will be sixty, so I would like to finally do some adventure. I got myself a speedboat for free, and I'm in the process of doing it up. I want to sail around Scotland, see a bit of my homeland. Money is tight, but it has always been that way. I reconciled myself many, many years ago to make the most of what I have. I will add pictures on social media and the like to let people see my progress.

I want to spend more time with my grandchild and enjoy teasing my children. It's my only sport. Ice been drafting a book on trauma-informed care. It would be nice for people to read it. I'm going to put it up for free when I'm finished.

I'd like to visit some of the places I've only read about- walk through the ruins of an old castle, feel the sea spray on my face from a different shore, get lost on a hiking trail somewhere Ice never been. There's a kind of magic in being a stranger to the world again, a kind of freedom in not having a past to carry around like a stone in your pocket.

I'm not chasing anything grand. I don't need a legacy. I'd be happy if I left behind a few good stories, a couple of jokes worth telling, and the sense that I made someone's day a little lighter. I'll still write, I'll just listen more to the wind, to the water, to the laughter of my grandchild as they grow up knowing only love. And just maybe I'll fade away into the night.

I have started writing, as well as this book, I'm in the process of drafting a three-novel epic fantasy. Two are already completed. I'm writing the other at the same time I am writing this. It's to keep me busy and to keep the demons away. They are in no way like this. This is about getting the memories out of my head and onto paper. It has been quite cathartic, and I'm enjoying the process. But by no means do I feel like an author.

In the next couple of years, I will be sixty, so I would like to finally do some adventure. I got myself a speedboat for free, and I'm in the process of doing it up. I want to sail around Scotland, see a bit of my homeland. Money is tight, but it has always been that way. I reconciled myself many, many years ago to make the most of what I have. I will add pictures on social media and the like to let people see my progress.

I'd like to visit some of the places Ice only read about walk through the ruins of an old castle, feel the sea spray on my face from a different shore, get lost on a hiking trail somewhere Ice never been. There's a kind of magic in being a stranger to the world again, a kind of freedom in not having a past to carry around like a stone in your pocket.

I'm not chasing anything grand. I don't need a legacy. I'd be happy if I left behind a few good stories, a couple of jokes worth telling, and the sense that I made someone's day a little lighter. I'll still write, I'll just listen more to the wind, to the water, to the laughter of my grandchild as they grow up knowing only love.

There's nothing quite like the sound of real laughter, the kind that starts as a small ripple and turns into a wave that knocks you over. I love those moments when a joke hits exactly right, and suddenly, you're all clutching your sides, tears streaming down your face, your breath coming in gasps. It's the best kind of pain, the kind that reminds you how good it is to be alive. Those moments are like lightning in a bottle unexpected, electric, and gone too soon. But they leave a glow behind, a reminder that even in the hardest times, joy is still there, waiting for its cue.

To anyone reading this who feels lost who feels like the storm will never end hold on. It will pass. You are stronger than you know, braver than you feel, and more loved than you can imagine. You are not alone.

I am still a storm child. But I am also the calm that follows. And that, I think, is enough.

The wind whispered through the trees, carrying with it the promise of spring. I sat on the edge of the garden, my back against the wall, my hand resting on the rough stone slab beneath me. The sharpness of the stone bit into my palms, but I didn't mind. The discomfort was grounding, a reminder of the present, of the here and now. I inhaled the rich aroma of coffee from my mug and took a sip, the warmth sliding down my throat, spreading through me. My breath clouded the air, dissipating into nothing just like so many of my friendships over the years. Faces and names, once vibrant and full of laughter, had faded like old photographs left too long in the sun. I had moved so many times, left behind so many streets, so many living rooms filled with the warmth of good company, that I had learned not to reach back. Not to hold on too tightly.

When I was young, I thought the world was an endless horizon of possibilities. Each new town brought the promise of fresh faces and potential friends. I would meet them, get to know them, and just as roots began to take hold, I'd be uprooted again. It was a cycle I learned to accept a lesson in impermanence.

Even now, seventy miles from what I considered home, I felt like a wanderer. There were connections faint threads on social media, the occasional message, a shared joke on a comment thread but nothing that filled the space where real companionship should be. My world had grown smaller, the circle tighter, until it was just me and that one close friend who had been a constant for the last twenty-eight years. Mark he listened when I was bouncing off the walls.

And Julie, of course, with her ever-branching friendships that filled the room with life and stories.

I admired that about her the way she could keep so many ties strong, how she seemed to effortlessly weave through life, leaving joy in her wake. I had never quite mastered that. I relied on her light to guide me through the fog of isolation, grateful for the warmth but always aware of the chill just beyond it.

It's not that I am lonely, not in the traditional sense. It's more like standing on a quiet shore, watching the waves roll in, knowing that beyond the horizon were ships and lands and bustling ports but I was content to just sit and watch. To let life pass by, a gentle tide against my feet, until one day I'd be pulled under, slipping into the night without a ripple to mark my passing.

I sighed; a sound lost in the wind and stood up. The garden slab left an imprint on my skin's temporary reminder of my time here. I dusted off my hands, turned away from the empty horizon, and walked back into the house. There was a kettle to boil, a boat to fix, and life to be lived quietly, but lived all the same.

And for now, that was enough.

In the end, it was a fitting epitaph for a life lived not grand, not gilded, but steady and real. A quiet ripple on the surface of a still lake, here and gone, but part of the water all the same.

A Note from the Author (Who Still Hesitates on the Shift Key)

I've spent most of this book trying to make sense of the storms I grew up in—and the ones I carried inside me long after the skies had cleared. I've written about pain, survival, resilience, and the strange quiet that follows a life lived looking over your shoulder. I've revisited things I buried so deep I forgot where I left them. But do you know what's still one of the hardest things to do?

Typing my own name.

With a capital letter.

It sounds silly, doesn't it? I can write about fists clenched at my side, about near drownings and broken codes of childhood, about betrayal and near-misses and moments that nearly shattered me—but when it comes to typing **Ian** with a proper capital *I*, I hesitate.

It feels... presumptuous. Like I'm announcing myself into a room I wasn't invited to. Somewhere along the way, I internalised the idea that I should stay small. Unseen. Silent.

And nothing says "sorry for existing" quite like slipping in a lowercase *I*, even when the rules say otherwise.

That's what this book has really been about. Not just survival—but unshrinking. Taking up space in a story I was told I didn't have the right to tell.

Writing *Storm Child* has been a bit like rooting through an old attic in the dark. I knew the ghosts were up there—I just didn't expect them to talk back. Or to leave fingerprints on the page. There were days I laughed at memories that should've broken me, and others where I cried over things I'd long forgotten I felt. Some of it's ugly. Some of it's raw. But it's mine.

And here's the thing—I wrote it.

Me. Ian. With a capital bloody *I*.

So, if you've made it this far, thank you. For listening. For witnessing. For holding the space, I wasn't sure I was allowed to occupy. It means more than I can say without sounding like I'm deflecting with humour again. Which, to be fair, I am.

But I'm learning.

Learning to sign my name like it belongs on the page.

Learning that survival is not just what happened *then*, but what I choose *now*.

Learning that sometimes healing looks like typing your name the way it was always meant to be.

Capitalised. This goes for all the storm children.

Glossary of Scots Terms

Aye: yes

Wee: small little

Aye: yeah

Daft: foolish, silly

Greet: to cry or weep

Div: a foolish person

Och: an expression of surprise, emotion, or dismissal Eh: a conversational tag, like, right? or you know?

About the Author

Ian Hughes is a Scottish writer whose voice blends raw truth with lyrical depth. *Storm Child* is their first and only memoir—a deeply personal account of surviving childhood trauma and navigating the long road to healing.

They are also the author of *The Echo of Fate* fantasy series and *The Elijah Hall Chronicles*, a historical fiction collection rooted in memory and resilience.

Though writing this memoir was difficult, Ian chose to share it in the hope that others might feel less alone.

When not writing, they can be found wandering the wild places of the world, collecting stories, and honouring the quiet courage it takes to survive.

☐ **dreamscapesunbound.uk**
☐ **Instagram: @ihughes88**

Support and Resources

If you have been affected by any of the themes in this book, please know that you are not alone. The following resources offer information, support, and community for those living with trauma, grief, neurodiversity, or mental health struggles.

Suicide Prevention

If you are struggling or someone you know is in crisis, help is available 24/7.

UK: Samaritans – Call 116 123 or visit www.samaritans.org
International: Find support at www.befrienders.org for global helplines
Text Support (UK): Text SHOUT to 85258 for free, confidential crisis support
SADS (Sudden Arrhythmic Death Syndrome)
www.sadsuk.org.uk – UK support for families affected by SADS
www.sads.org – U.S.-based information and advocacy

Autism and Neurodiversity

www.autism.org.uk – National Autistic Society (UK)
www.autistica.org.uk – Research and advocacy

www.neurodiversityweek.com – Celebrate and support neurodivergent lives

ACEs (Adverse Childhood Experiences)

CDC ACEs Info: www.cdc.gov/violenceprevention/aces UK Resources: www.youngminds.org.uk – Trauma-informed support for youth

Residential Care in the 1970s www.incaresurvivors.org.uk – For survivors of abuse in care www.future-pathways.co.uk – Support for adults abused or neglected in Scottish care www.mygov.scot/redress – Information about Scotland's redress scheme

Unstable Emotionally Personality Disorder (UEPD)

UEPD, often referred to as borderline personality disorder (BPD), involves patterns of intense emotional instability, fear of abandonment, impulsive behaviour, and deep interpersonal challenges. Though often misunderstood, recovery is possible with the right support.

www.mind.org.uk – Mind UK offers clear, supportive resources
www.personalitydisorder.org.uk – National Personality Disorder
Knowledge and Understanding Framework (UK)

Complex PTSD (C-PTSD)

C-PTSD can result from prolonged or repeated trauma, particularly in childhood, and includes symptoms of PTSD along with emotional dysregulation, low self-worth, and difficulties in relationships.

www.ptsduk.org – UK-based education and support for PTSD and C-PTSD www.outoftheshadows.today – Community for survivors of complex trauma

Depression

Depression can feel isolating, but it is also deeply common and treatable. You are not alone, and help is available.
www.depressionalliance.org
www.nhs.uk/mental-health – Information, symptoms, and treatment options www.mind.org.uk – Comprehensive resources and guidance

Historical Note: The Ice Cream Wars
Beginning in the mid-1970s, Glasgow's Ice Cream Wars were violent turf battles between gangs using ice cream vans to distribute drugs and stolen goods. The conflict escalated into tragedy with the arson attack that killed six members of the

Doyle family in 1984. It remains a defining moment in Scottish criminal and social history.

Further reading: The Ice Cream Wars (book by Campbell & Steele), BBC Archive, and www.crimeandjustice.org.uk Please remember: Recovery is not linear. There is no shame in seeking help. Your story matters. Your survival matters. And you are not alone.

Storm Child: A Trauma-Informed Reading Toolkit

Purpose:
This toolkit is designed to accompany the memoir *Storm Child* by Ian Hughes. It is intended for readers, book groups, educators, social workers, and trauma-informed care (TIC) professionals who wish to engage with the text on a deeper, more reflective level.

Storm Child is a powerful personal narrative of surviving the care system, childhood adversity, and loss. This toolkit integrates key principles of Trauma-Informed Care (TIC) to support readers in processing emotional responses, identifying moments of transformation, and drawing practical insights that can inform compassionate practice.

This document can be used independently or as part of a group discussion, continuing professional development (CPD) training, or reflective personal journaling. It serves as a bridge between lived experience and the professional frameworks designed to understand and support healing.

1. Trauma-Informed Lens: Core Principles

Safety
Storm Child explores environments where emotional and physical safety is compromised.
Reflection Prompt: Where in the memoir did the narrator begin to feel emotionally safe? What contributed to that?
Suggested Answer: Emotional safety begins to emerge during time spent with his grandfather and again in early moments of foster care when kindness is unexpectedly shown. Safety is often tied to presence, predictability, and people who listened without judgment.

Trustworthiness & Transparency
Readers witness the erosion of trust in both family and care systems.
Discussion Question: How does the author rebuild trust with the reader throughout the book?
Suggested Answer: By narrating events with brutal honesty and reflective self-awareness, the author creates a bond with the reader. He admits confusion, guilt, and longing without romanticising or exaggerating.

Peer Support
The narrator often finds comfort in siblings, friendships, and eventually partners.
Prompt: Identify scenes where connection helped the narrator survive or heal. How is peer support different from professional help?
Suggested Answer: His bond with his sister is essential in

the early years. Later, friendships and romantic relationships provide connection and belonging. These peer supports are based on mutual experience, unlike professional roles, which often lacked emotional closeness.

Empowerment & Choice

The memoir highlights many moments of disempowerment, especially in early life.
Activity: Note a turning point where the narrator begins to assert agency. What internal and external factors made this possible?
Suggested Answer: The decision to pursue higher education and health policy marks a reclaiming of agency. Factors include therapy, time away from destructive environments, and internal motivation to create change.

Cultural, Historical & Gender Awareness

The narrative is grounded in Scottish working-class life, layered with gendered and social class dynamics.
Discussion: How does identity (social class, culture, gender) shape the narrator's experiences of trauma and resilience?
Suggested Answer: The working-class context often silences emotional expression, especially among boys. Stigma around care, poverty, and masculinity compounds trauma. Yet identity also becomes a source of resilience and pride.

---

2. For Book Groups / Workshops

Discussion Guidelines (TIC-aligned):

- Speak from the "I" perspective.
- Everyone has the right to pass.
- Listen without needing to fix or solve.
- Assume complexity — avoid oversimplification of trauma.

Suggested Questions and Answers:

1. **What moment in the memoir stayed with you the longest, and why?**
   Answer: Many readers are struck by the chapter where the narrator leaves home with a bag of books and is not allowed to keep them — symbolising the erasure of identity.

2. **Which systems helped or harmed the narrator the most?**
   Answer: The care system often failed to protect, while individual social workers and educators occasionally became lifelines. The education system later became empowering.

3. **How does humour function as a survival strategy in the memoir?**
   Answer: Humour provides distance from pain, asserts control in chaos, and forges connection. It's also used to mask trauma when it becomes too much to face directly.

4. **Where did you see shame, and where did you see healing?**
   Answer: Shame is woven through early chapters —

in care, in family rejection, in silence. Healing begins through writing, reflection, education, and being loved without condition.

5. **What do you understand differently about childhood adversity after reading this?**
   Answer: That trauma is not just about what happens — but about what doesn't: the absence of love, safety, and validation. And that healing is never linear, but deeply human.

---

3. For Professionals (Social Work, Education, Mental Health)

Application Prompts and Suggestions:

- **How can this memoir inform your trauma-informed approach?**
  It highlights the lifelong impact of small moments — a word of kindness, a listening adult — and reminds professionals that presence matters more than perfection.

- **Where does the narrative illustrate TIC principles being absent?**
  Moments of forced separation, neglect in care, and dismissal of the narrator's emotional world show how systems often retraumatise instead of support.

- **What systemic failures are still relevant today?**
  Lack of continuity in care, underfunded services,

and stigma around mental health and care-experienced individuals remain ongoing issues.

Training Use: This book can serve as a case study to:

- Explore ACEs (Adverse Childhood Experiences) through narrative.
- Identify examples of complex trauma.
- Discuss long-term impacts and protective factors.

4. Additional Resources

Below are key tools and sources for deepening understanding of trauma-informed care:

- **UK Trauma Council (Resources and Frameworks):**
  https://uktraumacouncil.org/resources

- **Scottish Adverse Childhood Experience (ACE) Hub:**
  https://www.healthscotland.scot/population-health/child-adversity/adverse-childhood-experiences-aces

- **SAMHSA's Key Principles of a Trauma-Informed Approach:**
  https://ncsacw.samhsa.gov/userfiles/files/SAMHSA_Trauma.pdf

- **National Child Traumatic Stress Network (NCTSN):**
  https://www.nctsn.org/

- **ACEs Questionnaire and Guide:**
  https://acestoohigh.com/got-your-ace-score/

- **Beacon House Therapeutic Services – Free Trauma Resources:**
  https://beaconhouse.org.uk/resources/

- **Books and Research:**
  - *The Body Keeps the Score* by Bessel van der Kolk.
  - *What Happened to You?* by Bruce D. Perry & Oprah Winfrey
  - *In the Realm of Hungry Ghosts* by Dr. Gabor Maté

---

5. Contact & Permissions

To request group access to *Storm Child* for educational or training purposes, or to reach Ian Hughes for speaking or workshop opportunities, please contact:

Email: ianhughesska@gmail.com
Website: wwwdreamscapesunbound.uk

Storm Child: A Memoir by Ian Hughes — Raw. Resilient. Real.